MW00629159

AROMATHERAPY

AROMATHERAPY

From A Biblical Perspective

Ken McDonald B.D, Th.M.

First Edition

Copyright ©2018 Ken McDonald
All rights reserved.

ISBN: 978-1-942769-08-8

No part of this book may be used or reproduced in any manner whatsoever without written permission except in case of brief quotations embodied in critical articles and reviews.

This book contains the author's research sources, many of which are external website links. Those links are being provided to the reader as a convenience and for informational purposes only. They do not constitute an endorsement or approval by the author or publisher of any products, services, or opinions offered on the websites associated with those links, and the author and publisher bear no responsibility for the accuracy, legality, or content of those websites or for any affiliated links. Further, the author and publisher of this book expressly disclaim all liability for, and damages of any kind that may arise from the use of those links.

All Scripture quotes are from the
Authorized Version of 1611

Designed by Ken and Terri Lee McDonald
Cover photo used by permission from
www.shutterstock.com

www.kenmcdonaldfamily.com

Thank You

I would like to say thank you to some people that were instrumental in accomplishing the writing and publishing of this book:

 - Rich Clark for letting me write this book at his house.

 - Kathy Valance and her son, Arron, as well as Elaine Roscoe for the proof reading.

 - Jennifer, who kept asking for this book.

To my dear wife: Thank you, Terri Lee, for all of your support, feedback, and for being sober minded in regards to alternative medicine.

Other Books
By
Ken McDonald, Th.M.

Here Comes The Bride
A critique of the Baptist Bride Heresy

Pursuit
One Man's Quest to Find God's Perfect Will for His Life

Defiled
The Spiritual Dangers of Alternative Medicine

Jesus, Talk To Me
Have you ever wanted to get God's attention?
(Sermon in a Book Series, Vol. 1)

Dealing With Bad In-Laws
A Bible study on Jacob and Laban
(Sermon in a Book Series, Vol. 2)

Even As God
Healing Relationships Biblically
(Sermon in a Book Series, Vol. 3)

Good Vibrations
Overcoming Spasmodic Dysphonia
through vocal behavior exercises

Table of Contents

Preface

In the last 25 years, aromatherapy has become very popular in America. For centuries it has been used in other parts the world where there is little Biblical influence. But what does the Bible have to say about aromatherapy?

Proponents of aromatherapy will proclaim that essential oils are in the Bible and then proceed to give references where they are supposedly mentioned. Unfortunately, their misguided belief that the Bible is in agreement with aromatherapy causes some very serious spiritual problems. This misguided belief is one of the reasons that promted the writing of this book. The other reason serves to warn those who are unsure if they should use aromatherapy or not.

Let us look carefully into the word of God, the

Holy Bible, to see if the Bible and aromatherapy are in agreement, or is it just the opposite?

If it is the opposite, and the Holy Bible is contrary to aromatherapy, then there are many Christians who are grieving the Holy Spirit, as well as their Lord and Saviour, Jesus Christ, when they practice aromatherapy.

The foundational issue, as with all things pertaining to this life, is the question, "Does this grieve my Lord and Saviour Jesus Christ?" The only authority to determine if something does, or does not grieve the Lord, is the word of God. As a man, I am not an authority, nor is any man when it comes to this question. The inerrant word of God is the final authority in all matters of faith and practice. "**...Let God be true, and every man a liar.**"(Rom. 3:4) This fact gives you, the reader, liberty to search the scriptures to see for yourself, what the word of God says.

When determining what the scriptures teach, you must use them in their correct context and use them in their proper division.

> **15 Study to shew thyself approved unto God, a workman that needeth not to be ashamed, rightly dividing the word of truth. (2Timothy 2)**

See works by Clarence Larkin or C.I. Scofield, both of whom wrote in the early 1900's.

When I refer to the word of God, I am referring to a book that I hold in my hands and read everyday. I am not referring to some original manuscripts that noone alive today has ever seen, held, or read. I am referring to the Authorized Version of 1611, otherwise known as the old King James Version of 1611. That is the final authority.

With that understood, let's see what the word of God has to say about aromatherapy and the practices thereof.

Chapter 1

Aromatherapy

From the time I was nine years old, I have traveled the roads of America. As a young boy I would travel all over the west with my Grandmother each summer. Now, as an evangelist, I travel constantly all over America, as well as parts of the world. In these travels I see many things in various parts of this country.

I am partial to the western United States because I was raised in the Sierra Nevada Mountains of California, at 4000' elevation. In the summers I went backpacking into the Emigrant Wilderness area at 9000', and in order to get to Snow Lake, I had to hike over "Old Sammy" which was a mountain whose elevation was over 11000'. So there will always be a fond place in my heart for the western mountains.

When my wife, Terri, and I travel in the Eastern

United States, there is a little more history. The West is fairly "young." In the East it is a joy seeing the old buildings and experiencing places like Boston's Freedom Trail, New York's Empire State Building, and Philadelphia's Liberty Bell.

In the South it is a joy to see the sugar white sands of Destin, Florida contrasted with the turquoise waters, blue sky, and a beautiful red sunset. The colors there are fantastic, and the ocean waters are warm, not like the cold ocean waters of California I swam in as a child.

One day in particular and I am not sure exactly where we were, but I remember it was a place with many evergreen trees and hills. Not like the mountains in the West, but hills, so it probably was in the Northeast, around Pennsylvania. I was driving on a good country road lined with trees, when a building up the hill on my right caught my eye.

It was a one story modern house, but what caught my eye was the color of the siding on the house. It was clear coated with a natural wood finish, showing the wood grains, as well as the knots of the wood. It instantly reminded me of the homes up in the mountains of California! I thought it was a nice-looking house at first, then I saw the sign in front which read, "Aromatherapy."

I didn't say anything out loud, but remember thinking to myself, "Aromatherapy? What is that?" I thought, "Well, maybe it's a florist," but the

16

"Therapy" on the sign suggested that it was more than a mere florist. I don't know why, but I never forgot that day when "Aromatherapy " came to my attention.

Aromatherapy, sometimes written as aroma therapy, is just what the word proclaims. It is the use of scents, in the form of essential oils or incense, for therapeutic use. Therapeutic use means it is for the purposes of healing and helping the human condition.

As with many of the holistic healing practices, they date way back in time and have their origins in India, Egypt, China or Greece; with the majority of them from either India or China. The Shamanistic medicines of Acupuncture and Yoga are at the root of the vast majority of these practices. Yes, these practices have been studied and performed for thousands of years. Aromatherapy, in the form of incense, can be included in these medicines.

To be precise these medicines date back, biblically 5000 years. Why 5000 years? Because that is the timeline of history that dates back to Noah's flood. Only eight humans survived that flood and the vast majority of knowledge from before the flood was wiped out. Only recently has there been an uncovering of the civilization that existed before the flood. The archeological discoveries are fascinating. If you're interested you might get a book by Jonathan Grey titled, *Dead*

17

Men's Secrets.

As I cover the subject of aromatherapy, it will be from the point of view that the Bible is the inerrant word of God, and explains many things, that in other realms have neither light nor understanding. With the Bible, which is the word of God, the problem is not understanding what it says, but rather believing what it says. Briefly, let me give you an example of what I am talking about.

For centuries the following story has been attacked by skeptics, as well as Christian scholars alike, (I use the term Christian scholar loosely).

> **21 And Moses stretched out his hand over the sea; and the LORD caused the sea to go back by a strong east wind all that night, and made the sea dry land, and the waters were divided. 22 And <u>the children of Israel went into the midst of the sea upon the dry ground</u>: and the waters were a wall unto them on their right hand, and on their left. 23 And the Egyptians pursued, and went in after them to the midst of the sea, even all Pharaoh's horses, his chariots, and his horsemen. 24 And it came to pass, that in the morning watch the LORD looked unto the host of the Egyptians through the pillar of fire and of the**

cloud, and troubled the host of the Egyptians, 25 And <u>took off their chariot wheels</u>, that they drave them heavily: so that the Egyptians said, Let us flee from the face of Israel; for the LORD fighteth for them against the Egyptians. 26 And the LORD said unto Moses, Stretch out thine hand over the sea, that the waters may come again upon the Egyptians, upon their chariots, and upon their horsemen. 27 And Moses stretched forth his hand over the sea, and the sea returned to his strength when the morning appeared; and the Egyptians fled against it; and the LORD overthrew the Egyptians in the midst of the sea. 28 And the waters returned, and covered the chariots, and the horsemen, and all the host of Pharaoh that came into the sea after them; there remained not so much as one of them. (Exodus 14)

Here is an article declaring a satellite discovered the Red Sea crossing during the Desert Storm war: http://www.beforeus.com/satellite_redsea.html. Not only that, but all you have to do is google "Red Sea crossing" and you can see the underwater wreckage of Pharaoh's army. Included in the wreckage are chariot wheels that have been separated from the chariots. The design of the spokes on the wheels proves the timeline of events placing them on the exact time of the Exodus according to Nassif Mohammed Hassan, the director of Antiquities, Cairo, Egypt.

(https://wyattmuseum.com/discovering/red-sea-crossing - Significance of the wheels)

I find the archeological evidence fascinating, but we need to get back to the subject of aromatherapy.

For approximately 5000 years these shamanistic medical practices have been going on. They are nothing new, except to modern Americans. For the last 300 years America has had a very strong Bible influence, but as of 1901, the Laodicean period began, and the years of Bible influence have been subsiding. This worldwide condition was prophesied 2000 years ago by the Lord Jesus Christ, in Revelation 3, as well as foretold by the Apostle Paul in 2 Timothy 4. The Bible is always more up to date than the news. What is happening today in the world has not caught God by surprise. As a matter of fact, nothing ever catches God by surprise. Did it ever occur to you, that nothing ever occurred to God?

As this nation gets away from the Bible it is drawn back, not forward, backward into darkness. These holistic practices are nothing new. The Bible declares it this way, **"...there is no new thing under the sun."** (Ecc. 1:9) It may be argued that distillation processes were not invented until 400 years ago, but the Bible talks about distillation in

20

the book of Job 36:28, dating it around the time of Abraham.

At the root of aromatherapy is incense. Aromatherapy is nothing more than a form of incense, which has been used for 5000 years.

AROMATHERAPY INCENSE: AN AYURVEDIC TRADITION

One of the earliest known forms of aromatherapy comes to us from ancient India. It is the practice of burning and ambient inhalation of botanical essences and resins blended and rolled into incense according to ayurvedic tradition. Ayurveda, which literally means life-knowledge, is the ancient Indian art and science of healing and rejuvenation through the use of natural substances, such as herbs, roots, flowers, oils and minerals.

Although aromatherapy as it is practiced today relies primarily on the use of essential oils, this simple, traditional form of burning incense to release therapeutic fragrance is very much alive and well, and can be an inexpensive yet effective means of administering a variety of aroma-therapeutic benefits.

In massage therapy, incense is recommended as an alternative for those with skin sensitivities to the more commonly used forms of essential oils.

(https://www.massagemag.com/aromatherapy-incense-an-ayurvedic-tradition-10022/)

Incense Aromatherapy

We utilize the principles of both ancient and modern aromatherapy in the formulation of our incense blends to positively affect mind, mood, and cognitive function. The profound benefits of aromatherapy have been utilized for thousands of years and continue to aid in the greater healing process of humanity. For tens of thousands of years the burning, inhaling, or smelling of certain aromatic herbs, flowers, tree resins, gums, seeds, roots, barks, and oils has been used to heal the mind, body, and spirit. Incense has helped people from every walk of life on every continent attain to greater levels of well being, spiritual alignment, mental cognition, and emotional balance.

(https://highermindincense.com/our-vision/incense-aromatherapy/)

The Northwest School of Aromatic Medicine

Whether you are a community healer, family healer, or self-healer, the field of Aromatic Medicine is a universal modality that encompasses physiological, psychological, emotional, energetic, and spiritual health and wellbeing. **Incense and aromatics** have been used for millennia on every continent to heal the sick, balance emotional states, bring clarity to the mind, and **strengthen connection to spirit.** Those lucky enough to find themselves on the fragrant path are chosen representatives of the plant kingdom who are called to share the many gifts of beauty, healing, and true power of aromatics with the world.

The Northwest School of Aromatic Medicine is a unique conduit through which the sacred teachings of aromatic plants come to life. Through ancient fragrant traditions, ritualistic perspectives, and medicinal aromatic plant wisdom from around the world, aromatherapists, incense crafters, and herbalists will learn to strengthen their

23

foundational understanding and personal connection to aromatics and the plants themselves.

(https://aromaticmedicineschool.com)

The use of incense is very common in all of the mystic medicinal practices and traces back to the beginning of history. Whether the Vedas and the Hindu writings, or the Yellow Emperor and NeiJing of the Chinese writings, the holistic practices of today can be traced back to these two cultures. You will find the same practices to some degree or another in both of these cultures. Egypt, Greece and the American Indians are the other sources, but those cultures did not write it down the way the Hindus of India and the Taoists of China did.

The modern version of this age old practice of burning incense is to use essential oils. This is a subtle camouflage to make the gullible modern American think that it is something new. It is not! It is as old as any of the ancient practices. Aromatherapy uses incense, or essential oils to effect the human condition.

The majority of what we will cover in this book will be the use of essential oils. These "essential oils" are the main material substance used in aromatherapy today. These essential oils are infused, or atomized into the air and inhaled. They can be topically applied to the skin as well, or they can be ingested (i.e., eaten). Topical application and ingesting the oils are very delicate actions and sometimes cause damage to the person.

These supposed "safe all natural oils" can cause damage to your body. Why? Because at their root they are chemicals that have been refined out of the plants just like whiskey, vodka, or gin. The process of extracting the essential oils from the plants and materials they come from is usually by distillation. This makes the resulting product "spirits," just like distilled alcoholic drinks.

Some citrus plants have the oils mechanically expressed out of the skins, such as lemons and oranges. However, there are those who will request that even these oils be distilled, instead of expressed. I will explain why later in this book.

This begins our study of aromatherapy.

I laughed quietly to myself when I read the sign up on the hill. In my mind I pictured people sniffing things in order to be healed. To me, it seemed so foolish, and it is. Yet, to God and according to the word of God, this is very serious.

Aromatherapy

Chapter 2

Laying A Foundation

Should a Christian use Aromatherapy? Should a Christian use essential oils?

Perhaps the mere mention of these questions leaves you incredulous that such questions should even be asked. Perhaps you scoff at the notion that essential oils, and their use is even remotely wrong, let alone the possibility that it is a sin against God. Maybe you have seen "good" come out of using essential oils. You may know of people who have benefitted from the use of essential oils and Aromatherapy. But I ask you, "What does the Bible say?"

After all, the word of God is the final authority for as I mentioned in the Preface, **"Let God be true, and every man a liar."**(Rom. 3:4) The ONLY authority you should heed in the matters of faith and practice is the word of God. So I ask you, "If the word of God condemns the use of essential oils, will you accept it?" Perhaps you claim, "I don't trust you." Good, that is how you ought to be. But I am not the issue. The issue is, if the word of God is against aromatherapy will you side with the word of God?

There is many a person who is using aromatherapy, and to him/her it is utterly crazy to think that aromatherapy is wrong, or against the word of God. The use of essential oils seems so innocent. Just put a few drops of Lavender essential oil on a cotton ball and hold it up to your nose and inhale. There; Now you will be able to go to sleep. What's wrong with that? Oh, but the question should be, "What does the word of God say about that?"

16 This I say then, Walk in the Spirit, and ye shall not fulfil the lust of the flesh. 17 For the flesh lusteth against the Spirit, and the Spirit against the flesh: and these are contrary the one to the other: so that ye cannot do the things that ye would. 18 But if ye be led of the Spirit, ye are not under the law. 19 Now the works of the flesh are manifest, which are these; Adultery, fornication, uncleanness, lascivious-ness, 20 Idolatry, witchcraft, hatred,

variance, emulations, wrath, strife, seditions, heresies, 21 Envyings, murders, drunkenness, revellings, and such like: of the which I tell you before, as I have also told you in time past, that they which do such things shall not inherit the kingdom of God. (Galatians 5)

There are 18 things listed as works of the flesh. What is important to notice is that these are *works*. In the process of committing these sins; acts or works take place in their commission.

For example, let's take the first work of the flesh that is mentioned; adultery. There is no doubt that adultery is sin. It is a work of the flesh. That is very plain. In the commission of adultery there are works, or actions that take place when adultery is committed. At least one of the persons involved is married, and having sex with another person. The modern term is cheating on your spouse, and according to the Bible it is sin.

Can a born again Christian commit adultery? Yes! Is there ever a legitimate alibi for the commission of adultery? No! Should a born again Christian commit adultery? Absolutely not! While this is true a born again Christian is still living in a body of sinful flesh and can give in to the flesh just as a lost person.

According to the word of God a Christian has an

old man and a new man. Notice what the Bible says in Ephesians 4, which is written to Christians:

> **22 That ye put off concerning the former conversation the old man, which is corrupt according to the deceitful lusts; 23 And be renewed in the spirit of your mind; 24 And that ye put on the new man, which after God is created in righteousness and true holiness. (Ephesians 4)**

Jokingly, I want to say, "Now ladies, that does not mean you are to get rid of your husband. That is not the old man it is referring to." I then might hear some ladies reply, "Well, he is corrupt!" Ah yes! Aren't we all! If you are born again, won't it be great when we get our new bodies!

There is a battle that is constantly fought in a Christian between the old man and the new man, but you have a free will to choose which one you are going to obey. The old man says, "Choose my will." The new man says, "Choose my will." In your heart you choose which one you are going to serve. A lost person does not have this battle, but if you are saved, then you do. If you choose to commit adultery, you sin against God, and grieve the Holy Spirit that dwells inside of your body, who, by the way is also God the Holy Spirit.

Adultery is an act, and it is an act of the flesh

that lusts against the Holy Spirit. The lesson is this: "Don't do it!!!" It has nothing to do with the bed, or where it is done. Right? It has nothing to do with why you are doing it. Right? It has everything to do with "don't do it!" The work, the action that is adultery; don't do it. Regardless of where, how, why, or any other reason. The command is "don't do it!"

Why am I saying this? What is my point? As we study aromatherapy, the issue is not why one uses it. The issue is not how one uses it. Nor is it where one uses it. The issue is, what are the works of witchcraft? (Gal. 5:20) If aromatherapy is witchcraft, then don't do it! That's all there is to it. You see when you follow the word of God in this regard, it greatly simplifies things. **Works don't have to be figured out, they just have to be avoided.** There is no wiggle room.

Let me use one more as an illustration. In the list of the works of the flesh is the sin of murder. (Gal. 5:21) Can a saved, born again Christian commit murder? Yes! Again, in the commission of murder the issue is not what you used to kill someone. The issue is not how you killed someone. The issue is not why you killed someone. The issue is that you killed someone and thus committed murder.

If you are a Christian the command is the same: "Don't do that!" It applies for the lost just as well, but in the context I am trying to illustrate my reasoning here. The works of the flesh are works, and that is all you need to understand.

In recent years the world has abandoned absolute right and wrong and opted for situational ethics. By getting rid of God and adopting Darwin's illogical and unscientific theory of evolution, the world has opened the door to murder people under certain circumstances. However, the Bible still is true, God is still on the throne, murder is still murder, and Hell is still a place of fiery torments.

Perhaps you say, "What has this got to do with aromatherapy?" Simply stated, the Word of God defines works of the flesh, so that human attitude, opinion, and "slant" have nothing to do with it. Aromatherapy is a work of the flesh. The Word of God is very plain. That is why people don't want to read it. The vast majority of the time it condemns you and I. Thank God for the blood of Jesus Christ and a perfect salvation! Amen!

At the rudimentary level all you need to know is what the works are, and then as a child of God DON'T DO THEM!!! I emphasize this because when you get into the study of witchcraft there is a subtle temptation to focus on an object, instead of the act.

The Word of God calls these practices, "Curious Arts."

19 Many of them also which used curious arts brought their books together, and burned them before all

men: and they counted the price of
them, and found it fifty thousand
pieces of silver. 20 So mightily grew
the word of God and prevailed. (Acts 19)

These practices, or works, are called curious arts because of the subtlety of operation. They are curious to view, but you will never be able to figure out how or why they work. They are very curious, but the acts also seem so very innocent and "good."

Aromatherapy is a curious art. There will always be something about aromatherapy that man will never be able to explain physically. Various theories have been, and will be presented in order to explain how or why aromatherapy "works," but physically, man will never be able to absolutely explain how or why it works. To this day, there is no truly scientific evidence for the efficacy of aromatherapy physiologically, just as there is no true scientific evidence for the existence of disease as the result of a subluxation in the realm of Chiropractics. The Bible calls these metaphysical practices "curious arts."

In the art of Acupuncture there is a tendency to focus on the needle, the cupping, and the insertion of the needle, but that is only a deception to draw you away from what is really happening. It's not about the needle, it's about the act and the intercourse with the unclean spirit they call "Qi," pronounced "Chi."

Aromatherapy

So too, is it the same way with the curious art of aromatherapy and the use of essential oils. The temptation is to focus on the oils. How are they made? What do they consist of? Are they natural? As we delve further into this study, you will find that the issue is not the oils themselves. The issue concerns the works that are done with those oils. Who does these works?

As it is with adultery, it's not about the bed, couch, or floor. It's not about any number of other circumstances when the adultery was committed. It's about what was done; the act that took place.

By concentrating on what the word of God says, you avoid the subtle deception of focusing on an object, instead of the works. By doing this you are able to discern what is pleasing to the Lord Jesus Christ and the Holy Spirit. Pleasing the Lord, as well as submitting to the Holy Spirit, ought to be your prime aspiration in life.

When it comes to witchcraft, there are a number of diversions and counterfeits that show up to bring about confusion or justification of the acts. Whether it's the needles of acupuncture, the asanas of Yoga, the pills of homeopathy, the paralysis of muscle testing, or the iris of iridology, each one of these extraneous things diverts your attention from what it actually should be on, which is the works that are being performed. The same type of thing happens when Christians come to Galatians 5:20, and read the word "Witchcraft."

The average study of Galatians 5:20 ends up going to "the Greek" for the word "Witchcraft." That Greek word is φαρμεκια. The transliteration of this word is pharmekeia, which is translated as witchcraft, not pharmacy or drugs! The word of God is in English, not Greek! I am a Bible Believer and the word of God is preserved inerrantly, in English.

There seems to be a great avoidance of the word witchcraft by "Bible Believers." Even if they don't change it outright, they invariably mention that it is a reference to drugs. It's a strange thing to observe over the years, as I have sat in various Sunday Schools and classrooms and listened to Bible Believers as they taught the word of God. Automatically they shift when they come to the word, "witchcraft," and mention that it has to do with drugs. Very often they mention the Greek word Pharmekeia as proof for their statements as to the meaning and explanation of the word.

That creates a huge problem with this though because the words "drugs" or "pharmacy" are not even close to the same definition as witchcraft! The word of God says "witchcraft" and it means witchcraft, not drugs!

Pharmacies and drugs are not sinful. There has been many a pharmacy, as well as a drug, that has been an answer to prayer. Yes, they can be used by the Devil, but my point is that pharmacies and medical drugs are not sin.

Is taking aspirin a sin? Obviously no, it is not.

How about insulin? Is taking insulin sin? Of course not. Witchcraft is always sin, and witchcraft is always rebellion. To that there is no doubt!

> **22 And Samuel said, Hath the LORD as great delight in burnt offerings and sacrifices, as in obeying the voice of the LORD? Behold, to obey is better than sacrifice, and to hearken than the fat of rams. 23 For rebellion is as the sin of witchcraft, and stubbornness is as iniquity and idolatry. (1 Samuel 15)**

The problem is that many of the born again saints, whether preachers, teachers, evangelists, or any other saved sinners, have a hard time accepting the fact that a Christian can participate in witchcraft. So, what is witchcraft? Is it a Bible word? Obviously it is. Then you need to know what witchcraft is. If the word is included in the word of God, then you can safely assume God wants you to know what it means.

When I started studying holistic medicine, shamanism, acupuncture, yoga and the various types of eastern based medical practices, I did not know what witchcraft encompassed. At least not in the specific application, nor did I want to know what it involved. However, the more deeply I studied these subjects, the more I was confronted with the possibility of witchcraft being involved, so

I had to study the subject, as well as the practices involved in the workings of witchcraft.

Not limited to "witchcraft," the word of God has a few words along this line, such as divination, enchantments, sorcery, witch, familiar spirit, Diana, observer of times, astrologers, stargazers, monthly prognosticators, and wizards. These are all Bible words, and if you don't know what they are, then how can you be sure that you have not or are not getting seduced into committing these acts? Are you afraid of the truth?

Simple Concerning Evil

Please bear with me as I cover these various subjects before we actually get into the meat of the subject. This may seem tedious, but it is necessary.

In dealing with the subject of witchcraft oftentimes the command to be simple concerning evil comes up. Christians have used this verse wrongly to remain ignorant of many of the works of the Devil. Because of it they have fallen into sin and made shipwreck of their walk with God.

> **19 Yet I would have you wise unto that which is good, and simple concerning evil." (Romans 16)**

But to be "simple" concerning evil does not mean

to be ignorant concerning evil. Notice what it says in the book of Proverbs,

**3 A prudent man foreseeth the evil,
and hideth himself: but the simple pass
on, and are punished. (Proverbs 22)**

Obviously here in Proverbs, the simple is ignorant of the evil that is about to take place, but the prudent man recognizes the evil and avoids it. You are to be simple concerning evil but not ignorant of evil, but what does that mean? It means you are to study or examine evil, without participating in the evil. You are to judge righteous judgement based upon the word of God.

**15 But he that is spiritual judgeth all
things. (1 Corinthians 2)**

**24 Judge not according to the
appearance, but judge righteous
judgment. (John 7)**

To be "simple concerning evil" is to not partake in, or of the evil. At the same time examining it diligently, comparing the evil with what the word of God says.

Since the word of God is the law of righteousness, you are to be a judge in a courtroom. The judge does not participate in the actions. The judge hears the arguments and compares them with what the law says. Obviously in a jury trial, the jury becomes the judge. The judge then pronounces a sentence on the crime, if one was committed. When there is no jury, then the judge determines guilt or innocence and delivers the sentence based upon his verdict. In each example, however, the judge never participates in the crime. So too, a child of God is to judge all things by the word of God, without partaking or participating in the sin or evil. To participate is to no longer be simple concerning evil.

Years ago there was a preacher who did a slide presentation on rock and roll music. In his presentation he played clips of the music and then preached after each clip. That is not being "simple" concerning evil! There is enough evidence that rock and roll music is wrong and against God so that you do not have to play it. To listen to the music, and thus partake of the music causes one to no longer be "simple" concerning the evil that rock and roll music is. There is enough evidence that whiskey is wrong and against the word of God that you do not have to drink some to find out.

To be simple concerning evil does not mean to be ignorant. As long as you study, making a diligent comparison to what God said, then you are safe. (2 Tim. 2:15) When you participate in the evil, then you are no longer "simple" concerning the evil. Nevertheless, if you are ignorant of the evil, and fail to recognize the evil as evil then, instead of being prudent and avoiding evil, you will become deceived! **"pass on, and be punished."**

So as we get into the study of Aromatherapy and the use of essential oils, we will do it from the position and perspective of the word of God. We will examine it in light of what the word of God says, but we will not partake or experiment with it. There is no need for that.

> **130 The entrance of thy words giveth light; it giveth understanding unto the simple." (Psalms 119)**

Having laid a foundation on which to stand, we shall get into more particulars concerning the works of the flesh in regards to aromatherapy. According to the word of God it has to do with works.

> **16 This I say then, Walk in the Spirit, and ye shall not fulfil the lust of the flesh. 17 For the flesh lusteth against the Spirit, and the Spirit against the flesh: and these are contrary the one to the other: so that ye cannot do the things that ye would. (Galatians 5)**

So let's look at one of the works of witchcraft; aromatherapy, which is the use of essential oils or incense. Witchcraft covers much more than just aromatherapy, but there is no need to cover all the works of witchcraft. However there are two points about witchcraft that I want to make.

The first point is this. If you were to boil witchcraft (no pun intended) down to the very basic rudimentary level it is this: my will be done. In the practice of witchcraft, the raising of energy and the casting of spells, hexes, and mental projections, are all for the purpose of self. My will be done. Such a definition will fit to those who practice aromatherapy.

The other point in regards to witchcraft comes from the 1913 Webster's dictionary. It is a profound definition. Number 2 definition: **"Power more than natural."** That is it! The workings of Qi, Prana, or the "vibrational energy of the oils," brings about a metaphysical response. The results are beyond natural. They are supernatural.

Now, in regards to the works of witchcraft, let me be very specific. In the practice and performance of witchcraft, what do they do? What is used in order to practice witchcraft, and how is it used? They do not use a King James 1611 Bible when they practice witchcraft. You may laugh at that statement, but it is a very important point. They also do not sing hymns from a Christian Hymnal, nor do they pray to the Lord Jesus Christ, nor do they listen to sermons preached from the Bible. Those are works of Christianity, but those are not

Aromatherapy

works of witchcraft!

Do witches go to Walmart? Do they buy gas, drive cars, and wear shoes? Yes! But those acts and works are not what they do when they practice witchcraft! I am specifically referring to what they do when they practice witchcraft. Witchcraft is a work of the flesh, and those fleshy works lust against the Holy Spirit.

I can give example after example of saved, born again Christians who are doing the same works as the witches, for the same reasons and the same way. Off the top of my head, in my very limited sphere of operation, I could name five pastor's wives who are using and promoting witchcraft. I could name five pastors as well. In each case, whether the pastor's wife or the pastor, those ministries are failing. I was around some of the ministries before they got into the witchcraft, and the ministries were healthy and flourishing. Now they are dead and dying!

In this study of aromatherapy I will endeavor to follow this Bible admonition:

1 In the mouth of two or three witnesses shall every word be established. (2 Corinthians 13)

So I should have at least two witnesses, but I assure you I will have far more than that. It is not hard to find evidence and examples of aromatherapy and the use of essential oils being used in and for the purpose of practicing witchcraft.

I will try not to list so much as to cause the reading of such to be tedious. But please read all of the examples that I am going to show you as they illustrate the very heart of this argument and demonstrate for you, the reader, in a very clear way that aromatherapy and the use of essential oils is witchcraft and should be avoided by all who seek to please their Lord Jesus Christ as well as to not grieve the Holy Spirit.

The first testimony will be from a school for witches.

Witchschool.com

According to their website, as of 7/20/18:

> "271,426 people have registered as students of Witch School since September 4, 2001!"

That works out to be an average of 15,966 students each year, registering in the school for the last 17 years. That is about 44 students a day! Even so, come Lord Jesus!

The following is found in their course offerings:

Basic Aromatherapy
- Department: Default / Subject:

Herbology
- Open for Registration: All Registered Students
- Course Description:
- An introduction to the metaphysical uses of specific scents.

(http://www.classes.witchschool.com/course.asp)

This course offering is listed right after Athame 101.

What is an Athame?

According to the Official Witch Shoppe:

> On every Witch's/Wiccan's/Pagan's altar is an athame. An Athame is a double bladed knife often with a black handle that is used like a wand. It's point functions much like the top of a pyramid, energy concentrates at the blade tip and runs down both edges to the hand and arm of the person using it. Similarly, it can direct energy out of the body into the environment.
>
> (http://www.theofficialwitchshoppe.net/index.php?main_page=index&cPath=7)

So here is a school to teach people how to practice witchcraft and included in the course offerings is a class on Aromatherapy. Included in the list of classes further down the page is a class called,

Introduction to Aromatherapy - An exploration of the art of aromatherapy, the therapeutic use of scents.

(http://www.classes.witchschool.com/course.asp)

Not only do they teach on the magical use of scents, but included is a class on the therapeutic use of scents. This is the health side.

The next example of witchcraft is a website called spiritualspells.com. Their description of the website states:

Spiritual Spells provides information on Witchcraft, Wicca, and Hoodoo from an eclectic coven. A site for Witchcraft spirituality, guidance, and information on the Craft of the Wise.

The following is what they teach about essential oils. Please, consider the importance of what you are reading in relation to the word of God. This is very serious information.

"Spiritual oils, whether they be handcrafted herbal oils, ritual oils, condition oils, aromatherapy oils, or just pretty-smelling essential oils, are one of the largest and most varied of the ceremonial tools used in Witchcraft and Paganism."

"Spiritual oils are associated with the hidden fifth element of Spirit and help us reach out into the unseen ether and summon from it the forces we wish to communicate with or use in our rites and rituals."

"There are several basic kinds of oils that you might encounter in Witchcraft; these include ritual oils, condition oils, aromatherapy oils, essential oils and handcrafted oils."

"Synthetic Fragrance oils...A lot of companies today offer Synthetic Oils rather than Essential Oils because Synthetic Oils can be obtained at a fraction of the cost of Essential Oils. But, for magickal purposes it's always best to use real Essential Oils whenever possible, as these contain the magickal properties of the plant from which they are distilled, which the synthetic oils do not."

The following is included on the Spiritualspells website description of some of the essential oils they have. Notice the use of the word "work" and "workings" since we are talking about the works of the flesh.

"LAVENDER ESSENTIAL OIL This oil is best used for magickal workings relating to love and health work.

PATCHOULI ESSENTIAL OIL This oil is best used for magickal workings relating to money, and protection work, but it can also be used with great effectiveness for love and passion works.

CALAMUS ESSENTIAL OIL This oil is best used for magickal workings relating to gaining mastery and control through natural talent and charisma."

(http://www.spiritualspells.com/oils-book.html)

So far I have only given you two witnesses, but there is no doubt that based on just these two witnesses, the workings of witchcraft include the use of essential oils and Aromatherapy.

The following brief quotes are from the website. kitchenwiccan.com The founder of the website is Aldora Dawn. She is a witch, fortune teller, healer and Wiccan.

Aromatherapy has been a staple of spiritual practices for thousands of years.

Listed under the following heading:

Methods when making Concoctions for Wicca & Witchcraft;

47

Aromatherapy

Essential Oils (magical oils)
(https://www.kitchenwiccan.com/witchs-cup-board/apothecary/)

The spiritual practices referenced show Aromatherapy has been used in Witchcraft for thousands of years, hence the reference to essential oils being used to make concoctions to be used in Witchcraft.

The amount of information available, and relevant to this study is quite extensive, but it really would be too much, so I will try to be concise. Now consider the following quotes from the website: Dark Hollar Witch

> After choosing my herbs and roots or appropriate spell powder, I like to add essential oils to the wax. These oils are derived from herbs so their magical correspondences will be the same...As we know, aromatherapy is a distinct mind trigger that will help us during our spell. It's truly mind-blowing how aromatherapy plays its part in magic!
> (https://darkhollarwitchcraft.wordpress.com/2014/08/21/whats-in-your-candle-wax/)

Let me give you one last witness to the fact that Aromatherapy and the use of essential oils is

Witchcraft. The following quotes are from an author by the name of Scott Cunningham, who was initiated into Wicca under Raven Grimassi. Cunningham is dead now, having died at the age of thirty-six from AIDS complications, but the twenty-two books he authored are highly regarded in the realm of the occult and witchcraft.

> His books on Wicca led to a steady rise in his popularity, and he soon became one of the best-read Wiccan authors of his time. Sales of his most popular book Wicca: A Guide for the Solitary Practitioner (Llewellyn, 1988), reached over 400,000 copies by the year 2000   (http://www.controverscial.com/Scott Cunningham.htm)

The following quotes are from the book titled *Magical Aromatherapy: The Power of Scent*, Scott Cunningham, 1989, Llewellyn Publications

> Pg 3 - Similarly, when I wish to meditate, become involved in a relationship, increase my financial base or protect myself, I call upon the energies contained within essential oils and aromatic plants to manifest these changes through a process known as magic.

Aromatherapy

Pg 7 - The real force behind magical aromatherapy is found within scented plants and essential oils.

Pg 34 - In Magical aromatherapy, the use of true essential oils is mandatory. Synthetics won't work. Because essential oils are born of plants, they have a direct link with the Earth. This subtle energy, nourished by soil, Sun and rain, vibrates within essential oils. Since we too are of the Earth and also possess this link, we can merge the energy of true essential oils with our own to create needed change.

Essential oils are concentrated plant energies. In general, essential oils are from 50 to 100 times more concentrated than the plants from which they were taken. Therefore, essential oils are powerful reservoirs of natural energies.

Pg 35 - Synthetics, on the other hand, have no link with the Earth. In a magical sense, they're dead.

Pg 36 - Essential oils are so concentrated that one drop on a cotton ball is often all that is necessary for a effective magical aromatherapy ritual...

Pg 37 - True essential oils are vital to the practice of conventional, holistic aromatherapy.

Pg 187 - Glossary Definitions - Essential oil: Essential oils are fragrant, volatile substances produced by certain types of plants. In a sense, they are the "blood" of the plant, the manifestation of the life force which created it. In magical aromatherapy, the term usually refers to the liquids themselves, freed from the plants which created them. These natural aromas are the key tools in aromatherapy.

Pg 189 - Synthetic "essential" Oils: Synthetic scents are useless in both magical aromatherapy and its conventional cousin (holistic aromatherapy) and shouldn't be used for these purposes under any circumstances.

Though lengthy in my quotes, yet I have quoted from only six witnesses, but these six witnesses prove that Aromatherapy and the use of essential oils is, and are, one of the tools used extensively by witches in the practice of witchcraft.

Let me stress one more time that the witches do

not do the works of Christianity, in that they are not using a King James 1611 Bible, singing from a hymnal, praying to Jesus Christ, or attending Bible believing churches. It is the Christians that are doing the same works as the witches are doing, the same ways, for the same reasons. A major reason Christians use them is for healing, which the witches do as well, although they also use them for mood altering effects.

> 16 This I say then, Walk in the Spirit, and ye shall not fulfil the lust of the flesh. 17 For the flesh lusteth against the Spirit, and the Spirit against the flesh: and these are contrary the one to the other: so that ye cannot do the things that ye would. 18 But if ye be led of the Spirit, ye are not under the law. 19 Now the works of the flesh are manifest, which are these; Adultery, fornication, uncleanness, lasciviousness, 20 Idolatry, witchcraft, hatred, variance, emulations, wrath, strife, seditions, heresies, 21 Envyings, murders, drunkenness, revellings, and such like: of the which I tell you before, as I have also told you in time past, that they which do such things shall not inherit the kingdom of God. (Galatians 5)

Chapter 3

Quintessential

The term essential oil comes from "quintessential oil," which stems from the Aristotelian concept of the fifth element, after fire, air, earth, and water. As described by the National Association for Holistic Aromatherapy, one of the two governing bodies for national educational standards for aromatherapists:

> The fifth element, or quintessence, was then considered to be spirit or life force. Distillation and evaporation were thought to be processes of removing the spirit from the plant and this is also reflected in our language since the term "spirits" is used to describe distilled alcoholic beverages such as brandy, whiskey, and eau de vie.
> (https://www.treehugger.com/health/13-essential-oils-and-what-theyre-good.html)

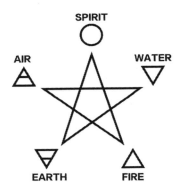

**WICCAN Orientation of Pentagram
with spirit on top
Alchemy symbols included**

Orientation of Pentagram

The Church of Satan decided on a point-down orientation. This allows them to place the goat-head within the figure. In addition, according to writers such as Levi, this was the "infernal" orientation, and thus seemed the appropriate orientation for Satanism. Finally, the point-down figure represents spirit subsumed by the four physical elements, rejecting the notion that the physical world is dirty and taboo and that the spirit should rise about it.

(https://www.thoughtco.com/pentagrams-4123031, by Catherine Beyer, Updated October 24, 2017)

There is truth in the thought of the essential oils possessing the spirit, or that they are spirit oils. Aromatherapy claims that the essential oils get their power or energy from the plants. It is purported that they capture the life of the plant, or the essence of the plant; that the oils are actually alive. It is this "life" that is used in witchcraft or aromatherapy for the purpose of accomplishing healing or casting a spell. This "life" of the spirit oils is a metaphysical entity and thus it is spirit.

The belief of capturing the life or spirit of the plant began many years ago. As with many of the occult works, the early evidences can be traced back to either India, China or Egypt. It usually traces back to one of those three and sometimes Greece is mentioned, but Greece is mostly mentioned when dealing with giants, wisdom, the Greek gods, and the fallen angels.

When it comes to medicine, health and healing, it traces back to China with *The Yellow Emperor's Classic; Nei Jing*, or to Ayurveda of Hinduism, or to Egypt. Although in Egypt there is no single book, but rather an eclectic collection of writings and hieroglyphs from which various medical practices have been gleaned. Historians estimate date back to about 2500 to 3000 years BC.

Do you know why it dates back approximately that far? Because 2500 to 3000 BC is the time right after the flood. *The Yellow Emperor's Classic* dates back approximately 2500 years BC. The book contains a story about the Emperor and his medical authority named "Qi-bo," to whom he would ask questions. Tradition teaches that Qi-bo learned medicine from an ethereal being. In the first recorded dialogue between the Yellow Emperor and Qi-bo the conversation begins with the Yellow Emperor asking:

> "I have heard that the people of ancient times lived as long as one hundred and twenty years with no signs of weakening in their movements at that age. But people nowadays become weakened in their movements at the age of less than sixty years old. Is this due to change in natural environments or due to man's faults?"
>
> (The Yellow Emperor's Classic of internal Medicine, translated by Dr. Henry lu, Vancouver, BC, Published by international College of Traditional Chinese Medicine of Vancouver, BC, 2004, Su-Wen, Chapter 1, s1-2)

Well, my, my, my! Here is a Chinese emperor over 4,600 years ago who was aware that people used to live longer, but now they didn't live as long. If you know your Bible you know that the Lord decreed that man would live no longer than 120 years, at the max, when before the flood they were living over 900 years. And this emperor wants to know if it is due to Nature, or man's faults. The other word for faults is, Oh my, not that word, it's such a horrible word, oh, no! The word is. . . SIN!

(DEFILED, Every Word Publishing, Ken McDonald, pg 130)

Whether Indian, Chinese, or Egyptian, the knowledge is going to date back about that far. They don't know why, but if one has the word of God, then one knows exactly why. Any knowledge that is claimed older will be such as is attributed to Qi-bo; that he obtained it from an ethereal being. Ethereal being is another word for a devil, or fallen angel.

When it comes to essential oils, the history does not go back nearly that far. It goes back to a man by the name of Paracelsus. He was a mean drunk, and a practicing astrologer. He believed in the use of Talismans, which are charms or stones that have the power to work miracles.

(https://www.oilsandplants.com/paracelsus.htm)

Distillation being a means of separating the essential from the crude and non-essential with the help of fire, it met in an almost ideal way the definition of a "chymical" process valid until about the end of the seventeenth century and given a special meaning by the great Swiss medical reformer, Bombastus Paracelsus von Hohenheim (1493-1541). His theory was that it is the last possible and most sublime extractive, the Quinta essentia (quintessence) which represents the efficient part of every drug, and that the isolation of this extractive should be the goal of pharmacy.

This theory undoubtedly laid the basis for research in the preparation of essential oils after this time. The very name "essential" oils recalls the Paracelsian concept—the Quinta essentia.

(The Essential Oils - Vol. 1: History - Origin in Plants - Production - Analysis, Fred Guenther, Jepson Press, March 15, 2007, ISBN-13: 978-1406703658)

Quinta Essentia... it is the life of the object from which it is extracted in the form of fluid... it is the soul of the object."

(Paracelsus: An Introduction to Philosophical Medicine in the Era of the Renaissanc, 2nd, revised edition, Basel; New York: Karger, 1982, By Walter Pagel, pg 100)

The term "essential oil" is a contraction of the original "quintessential oil." This stems from the Aristotelian idea that matter is composed of four elements, namely, fire, air, earth, and water. The fifth element, or quintessence, was then considered to be spirit or life force.

(The National Association for Holistic Aromatherapy, https://naha.org/explore-aromatherapy/about-aromatherapy/what-are-essential-oils)

In the Alchemy writings of old the quest was to find the quintessence of life. This quintessence, if you boil it right down to the nitty gritty, was the quest to find the fountain of youth, or eternal life. What they were trying to obtain was a way to live forever, without having to repent and call upon Jesus Christ for their salvation. At the root of Alchemy is rebellion plain and simple.

In Wicca, the quintessence is the top of the point of the star, when the star is pointing upward. In Satanism, the quintessence is this same point, yet it is pointed infernally or downward towards the earth.

Notice that in both instances the star refers to the alchemical elements of fire, water, earth, air, and the fifth element is spirit/aether. This fifth element has over 100 names, from Chi, Prana, Manitou, Innate intelligence of chiropractic, elixir, kundalini of Yoga, and I could go on and on. But the greatest clue as to what the quintessence is, is found in the name quintessence, or fifth element.

You see, at one time in Heaven there were five Cherubim/Beasts around the throne of God. There were four, with one stationed at each corner of God's throne, and there was one more cherub; it was the fifth cherub that was above the throne of God. This cherub was Lucifer.

> 8 And the four beasts had each of them six wings about him; and they were full of eyes within: and they rest not day and night, saying, Holy, holy, holy, Lord God Almighty, which was, and is, and is to come. (Revelation 4)

> 14 Thou art the <u>anointed cherub that covereth</u>; and I have set thee so: thou wast upon the holy mountain of God; thou hast walked up and down in the midst of the stones of fire. 15 Thou wast perfect in thy ways from the day that thou wast <u>created</u>, till iniquity was found in thee. 16 By the multitude of thy merchandise they have filled the midst of thee with violence, and thou hast sinned:

therefore I will cast thee as profane out of the mountain of God: and I will destroy thee, O <u>covering cherub</u>, from the midst of the stones of fire. 17 Thine heart was lifted up because of thy beauty, thou hast corrupted thy wisdom by reason of thy brightness: I will cast thee to the ground, I will lay thee before kings, that they may behold thee. (Ezekiel 28)

Notice the word, "anointed." To be physically anointed in the Bible was to have oil poured or rubbed on you, usually at a dedication for a spiritual office, such as a priest.

Webster 1913, "1. **To smear or rub over with oil**... " Therefore when essential oils are applied topically it is a form of anointing someone, or they are anointing themselves.

To be spiritually anointed in the Bible was to receive, or to have, the Holy Spirit. Jesus Christ is the anointed of God, the Messiah, the Christ. (Isa. 61:1 & Luke 4:18, Acts 4:27, 10:38).

Christians are said to be anointed as well.

21 Now he which stablisheth us with you in Christ, and hath anointed us, is God; 22 Who hath also sealed us, and given the earnest of the Spirit in our hearts. (2 Corinthians 1)

Aromatherapy

To be anointed spiritually is to be a "christ." Jesus is the Christ. Those who are born again and thus in-dwelt by the Holy Spirit have been anointed, hence we are called Christ-ians. We are little anointed ones (i.e., Christians).

Lucifer was anointed thus making him a christ. (Eze. 28:14) Then, he was a christ, but now, after his fall, he is an anti-christ. He was also a cherub. The face of a cherub is an ox, or a calf. (Compare the faces with Eze. 1:10, and Eze 10:14, and Rev. 4:7).

This "fifth" cherub was over the throne of God. In Revelation 4 there are four beasts otherwise known as cherubim. Originally there were five, with Lucifer over the throne. He was anointed making him the highest, most powerful created being and office in all of Heaven. **"And I have set thee so."** He was the fifth cherub and his face is that of an Ox. This fifth element that no one seems to be able to define is Lucifer, and the Bible says that:

> **2 Wherein in time past ye walked according to the course of this world, according to the <u>prince of the power of the air</u>, the spirit that now worketh in the children of disobedience... (Ephesians 2)**

> **4 In whom the <u>god of this world</u> hath blinded the minds of them which believe not, lest the light of the**

glorious gospel of Christ, who is the image of God, should shine unto them. (2 Corinthians 4)

It is amazing what happens when someone will just believe the word of God! Lucifer, who was once a cherub, the fifth cherub that covered the throne of God, is now a serpent dragon, (Job 41, Rev 12, Dragon, in your King James Bible means dragon! It does not mean dinosaur.) the one the Chinese worship and the god of this world. Who also, as a spirit, works in those who have never been born again. The "fifth element" is Lucifer, AKA Satan or the Devil.

He is the god of this world, and the prince of the power of the air. Isn't that a strange statement, the prince of the power of the air? This is very important.

The air has power in it. The Chinese know this. The purpose of Qigong is to bring that power into their bodies, usually for health and longevity. To use the power of the air for healing is to go to Satan for your healing. For a Christian to do this is called spiritual adultery because you are having intercourse with an unclean spirit.

> Webster 1913: witchcraft: 1. The practices or art of witches; sorcery; enchantments; intercourse with evil spirits.

Jesus Christ is called, **"the Prince of Peace"** in Isaiah 9:6. So all true peace comes from Jesus Christ. Anything else is counterfeit and not true peace. True lasting peace is impossible without righteousness. Jesus Christ is righteous and all; I said, "all," there is nowhere else to go, all real peace comes from and through the Lord Jesus Christ.

With that being said, Satan is, **"...the prince of the power of the air."** (Eph 2). Any power that comes from and through the air is Satanic.

Martial arts' power is satanic. Amen! See Bill Rudge's pamphlet: *Why I quit Karate.* Bill Rudge is the founder of the Christian Martial Arts Association, and he resigned because he realized that Karate is witchcraft and against the Lord Jesus Christ.

Essential oils, which were originally termed, "Quint essential oils" are spirits in that they have passed through the air in the process of being created. As they pass through the air there is a power that connects to them.

I can hear them screaming , "No, no, no! You got it all wrong. Through distillation they are capturing the life force of the plant. The power comes from the plants in that they are capturing the life energy of the plant."

Well, that is what the holistic healer crowds believe, but the problem is there is no absolute evidence to the veracity of that proclamation. If that is true, then that may explain the different uses or purposes for each essential oil, but when it is proclaimed that there is "life force" in the oils, and that the essential oils are alive, then that meta-physical energy is from the prince of the power of the air. The life force energy came from the air. It is the quintessential power, the fifth element, just like the fifth cherub. (Eze. 28). Essential oils are sometimes referred to as, "Qi in a bottle." (http://aromaqigong.com/qiblog/)

Palo Santo essential oils come from the Palo Santo tree of South America. But there is one thing you ought to know about the harvesting of the wood. They only harvest the wood from a naturally fallen Palo Santo tree. The following is a quote from a Palo Santo supply Company:

> "An ideal aging process involves a naturally fallen tree aged a minimum of three to five years, and often up to 10 years."
>
> (https://palosantosupply.co/blogs/palo-santo/116334723-your-guide-to-palo-santo-an-introduction)

> It is believed that a tree or fallen branches must lie dead for 4-10 years before the medicinal and mystical properties of the wood begin to come alive. It is also believed that the branches of the Palo Santo that are

felled by lightning have the highest concentration of medicinal and mystical properties.

(https://www.mountainroseherbs.com/produc ts/palo-santo-smudge-sticks/profile)

So the wood the essential oils are distilled from is dead! There is no life in it, yet Palo Santo is a major essential oil for spiritual workings and magic. It is a very powerful essential oil, but it comes from a dead tree that has been laying on the forest floor for up to ten years. The oils may be enhanced with age, but there is no life in the wood so whatever power is in the essential oils it can not be attributed to the life of the tree, for the life of the tree expired ten years earlier. The power, or life force, or fifth element, comes from the air it passes through when it is distilled. It gets its power when it turns into a spirit, and that power is from the prince of the power of the air whose name is Satan.

21 There is no peace, saith my God, to the wicked. (Isaiah 57)

All true peace begins with the Lord Jesus Christ. He is the source, the supplier, and the sustainer of peace. The headwaters of peace begin to flow with the Lord Jesus Christ, and that river will never dry up! Just as Jesus Christ is the source of all true peace in this life and world, so too is Satan the prince and the power of the air.

The vast majority of Essential oils are spirits, for they have been distilled. That means they have passed through the air and condensed on the other side of their passage. If any power was gained, then according to the word of God, it came from Satan.

This is the reason synthetic essential oils don't have any power. Synthetic essential oils have never been distilled. They have never vaporized and passed through the air. The are energetically dead oils. Witches do not like nor use synthetic essential oils for this reason.

Many Native Americans claim that whiskey, (a spirit) has a devil in it. In Tennessee for years booze was referred to as the devil's drink. And it still is! Jesus Christ said,

> **10 The thief cometh not, but for to steal, and to kill, and to destroy: I am come that they might have life, and that they might have it more abundantly. (John 10)**

While I am here, there is one thing for sure and that is "spirits" like whiskey, vodka, and gin have destroyed countless homes and lives around the world. They are called "spirits" just like the Quintessence spirits. The fruits of both are stolen purity, the killing of innocent lives, and the destructions of homes and families. I can give you examples for either booze, or aromatherapy. The results are the same except one works spiritually, and the other works physically, but they both are out of the pit of Hell!

Attorney David Gibbs tells the story of how one Sunday morning he was sitting on the platform in an auditorium of a large church. As the choir came in and assembled behind him on the platform, simultaneously he watched two men carry another, very crippled, and deformed man, into the auditorium, setting him in a special chair designated specifically for him. The severity of the man's disfigurement necessitated the two ushers to lock arms, forming a cradle, in order to carry him into the church auditorium.

As the church service began Bro. Gibbs said that he found himself wanting to look at this crippled man, but not wanting to stare. He had never, in all of his lifetime, seen a man with a more unusual body than this man, and then he began to describe the man that he saw that day.

His arms were attached to his body in a cork screw fashion. They were completely twisted around an entire revolution and half bent, stuck out from his body like a bird's wings that were not all the way withdrawn. His legs were the same way: corkscrewed. One leg was fully a foot shorter than the other. His right leg ended with his toe pointing perpendicular. On his left leg, the heel was in front, and his toes pointed backwards. His body was scrunched. Most tragically was his face.

Attorney Gibbs went on stating that everyone here tonight has a beautifully bowed face, but this crippled man's face wasn't flat. Conversely, his face was caved inward. His teeth protruded out farther than any other feature of prominence on his face. So David Gibbs began to ask the pastor about the deformed man, and this is the story he told.

The crippled man was not born that way. Twenty three years earlier that young man was born perfectly normal. Two years after he was born, his father, a big strong man, went out drinking one night with a bunch of his buddies and got drunk. That drunken sot of a man came back to the house where the two year old boy and his mother were sleeping.

That drunken man with his buddies beat on the door and wanted to come in. The mother came to the door and protested his bringing his drunken friends into the house, especially with bottles in their hands. Because the father was not allowed admittance, he grabbed the mother by the throat and began to hit her in the face repeatedly. He beat her bloody and knocked her unconscious. He then let her fall on the floor motionless. Now these drunken men had the run of the house.

They went to the little two year old boy's bedroom and got him out of his crib in his little pajamas. They carried him into the living room, and when the little boy saw his mother bloodied and unconscious on the floor he began to scream hysterically.

The drunken men, to quiet him, played with him. What they did was unthinkable. They took the little boy by an arm, and whirled him overhead. Joints began to split and snap. The little boy screamed, but in their drunkenness, all they needed was to play a little longer.

So by the other arm, they whirled him overhead. With both arms and legs mangled and twisted, they began to toss him one to another and dropped him again and again on his head. Eventually, and mercifully, the little boy went unconscious.

In the morning when they awoke from their drunken stupor, miraculously, the little guy had not died. They were so terrified, for they knew that they could go to prison for what they had done, hence, they never took him to a doctor.

The pastor then ended the story with this

statement: "What is parked down here in front of you in this auditorium is one drunken night of abuse."

Some Indians claim there is a devil in each bottle. Spirits! Whiskey, Vodka, Gin, etc. are spirits. In the distillation process the liquid evaporates (becomes a vapor) and passes through the air. It then cools and condenses on the other side, in the coils of the distillery. Next it trickles into a container, but they are called spirits because they pass through the air. During the process, they vaporize, just like the majority of essential oils do when they are distilled.

I say "majority" of the essential oils because more often than not, citrus oils are not distilled. They are expeller pressed. It's important to note that there are people who in the use of essential oils state that all oils for use should be distilled, even the citrus oils. Do you know how you can tell if citrus oils are distilled?

It is my understanding that the distilled citrus oils do not create photo toxicity. In other words, expeller oils can cause you to get burned if you go out in the sun after topically applying them. Distilled citrus oils do not do that. Not only that, but according to floracopeia.com, "Most of the phototoxic oils are also photocarcinogenic." That's right! They can cause cancer when exposed to the sun. When is the last time you read that? Oh, but they're natural. They're safe and natural. Really?

Even more obvious though is the fact that the method of choice for the use of essential oils is to infuse the volatile oils into the air. Therefore, any power they have has come from Satan. The citrus oils are recommended to be distilled so they are cleaner and safer to use.

The very nature of the term "aroma therapy" declares that the method of therapy is by aroma, thus through the air. Therefore, according to the word of God, if they have any power their source for that power is Satan. Not only that, but again its very nature "aroma therapy" is spiritual because it is an airborne therapy. Most of the time the oils are inhaled through the nostrils. This puts it on a spiritual plain.

> **7 And the LORD God formed man of the dust of the ground, and breathed into his nostrils the breath of life; and man became a living soul. (Genesis 2)**

Body = Dust of the ground
Spirit = Breathed into his nostrils the breath of life
Soul = Man became a living soul
Your spirit has to do with the movement of air

through your nostrils AKA breathing.

> Webster 1913: spirit - 1. Air set in motion by breathing; breath; hence, sometimes, life itself.

The Bible says, "...the body without the spirit is dead." (James 2) If you do not have the movement of air passing through your lungs, and usually through the nostrils, then you are dead.

Your body is sustained through the process of respiration, the movement of air in and out of your body. God designed you that way. Respiration is not the same as the gathering of power from the air. Respiration was ordained and designed by God, but the gathering and directing of power from the air is controlled by Satan. At least that is what the Bible states. He is, "...the prince of the power of the air." (Ephesians 2:2)

Aromatherapy

Chapter 4

Christians
Doing Witchcraft

The church service had gone well. The singing, preaching and formal church activities were done and now people were hanging around talking, fellowshipping and having a good time.

A couple of ladies came over to me and had questions about Holistic medicine. They were particularly interested in my thoughts concerning the treatments that they were doing. Most of the time, people will not discuss New Age Medicine with me, but now and then they do, which I enjoy as it gives me another window of understanding of how they view New Age Medicine. Most of the time their views are quite similar, but now and then, there is a difference in their viewpoint.

As these ladies began to question me, I explained specifically the problems with what they were doing. In particular one was using Aromatherapy, and the other was using Homeopathy. They did not like my answers and kept coming back with, "But what about..."

Finally and politely, at least I believe I was being polite, I responded by saying, "The works that witches do, when they practice witchcraft...don't do that. I can show you witches that are doing the same thing that you are doing, for the same reason, the same way. You are not to do that according to Galatians 5."

Their frustration began to increase when one of them blurted out, "Well, I don't worship the Devil. That's not why I do what I do," and then she left. It was obvious that she did not know what witchcraft is.

Wicca is only one form of witchcraft, much like Southern Baptists are only one form of Baptists. The majority of witches would readily proclaim that they do not worship Satan either. As a matter of fact many don't even believe in a literal devil or Satan, (that just shows how deceived they really are). They believe in the god and goddess, such as Diana in Acts 19.

You see, the problem is that when I show people, or declare to them that aromatherapy is witchcraft, they do not believe that what they are doing is witchcraft. Just the mere thought of a Christian practicing witchcraft seems ludicrous. Yet, in this Laodicean age in which we live, there is now out in the open what is termed, "Christian Witchcraft."

But for the ladies, usually it's ladies who are saved, in church, and claim to love the Lord Jesus Christ, they can't wrap their mind around the fact that they are practicing witchcraft. I am confindent that the average saved Christian lady who is using witchcraft, is doing so out of a sincere heart of love to help others and to heal. Many are performing these works seeking to be a help and a blessing to others, especially their own family. So when they are confronted with the fact that it is witchcraft they can't fathom such a thought. It seems preposterous to them. I will admit that as I began to study the New Age Medicine, it just seemed like good natural medicine.

Following much prayer and studying God's word, the light began to dawn upon me as I saw the word "witchcraft" in Galatians 5! I started to study the actions and practices of witches, and what they did when they practiced witchcraft, and it was then that I saw the connection of the two.

I remember researching the actions of the witches, and saw the essential oils for sale in the Witches' supply shops. That stunned me, as it was very plain to see. Then I saw that they were infusing them, just like the preachers' wives that I knew were infusing, and it was for the same reasons. It was for health, and many of the same essential oils were being used for the exact same problems.

Aromatherapy

I was amazed, astonished, and stunned when I saw the identical works being done in the Christian realm as it was being done in the realm of the witches. I pushed back from the table where I was viewing my computer screen, stood up with my eyes wide with wonder and my mouth dropped open, and almost in a whisper I said, "They're doing the same things that the witches are doing! They...they... they're practicing witchcraft!"

And then I realized, "I...I...have been using and practicing witchcraft!" I moved to my bedroom, and kneeling at my bedside, even though I had already repented some months earlier, yet upon the realization of what I had been doing, it broke my heart. There beside my bed I confessed my sin again, and wept before my Lord Jesus Christ and got things right.

I have not shown you all that the witches do when they practice witchcraft, and it is not necessary to do so. I implore you to understand that included in the practice of witchcraft is the use of essential oils and Aromatherapy. It is part of the works that witches do when they practice witchcraft. They infuse oils, natural essential oils, into the air so that the air will become charged with their scent and power, so that whatever the expected intention, it will succeed.

In some places, and centuries ago the method was to burn incense. This is still a form of aromatherapy used today. The burning of incense is popular in aromatherapy as well as in witchcraft. One of the reasons is because it is cheap and easily made at home.

Incense, as well as essential oils are commonly used for the casting of spells. Oh, you may say, I don't do that! But you have blends of oils for specific expected results, do you not? You infuse them into the air for an intended purpose to take place.

Forgive, by doTerra:

> The fresh, woody aroma of doTERRA Forgive Renewing Blend helps to counteract emotions of anger and guilt, while promoting the liberating feelings of contentment, relief, and patience. (https://www.doterra.com/US/en/p/forgiveren ewing-blend-oil)

If you are having emotions of anger and guilt it is a sin for a born again Christian to use essential oils to help get the victory over these things. Yes, I said it is a sin. Why? Because the Bible way is to spend some time in private prayer with the Lord Jesus Christ, ask foregiveness for your sin, and get your heart right with God.

Perhaps your guilt is the Holy Spirit dealing with you about sin in your life. But instead of going to the Lord Jesus Christ in prayer, you infuse these essential oils and the unclean spirit that is associated with the use of these oils calms and comforts you so that you can, "Forgive yourself." There you now feel so much better, but the feeling won't last because you still have not gotten right with God. As a matter of fact, by using the essential oils you are getting further and further away from God.

Forgiveness, by Young Living:

Description: "Forgiveness™ contains an aroma that supports the ability to forgive yourself and others while letting go of negative emotions, an important part of personal growth.

(https://www.youngliving.com/en_US/products/forgiveness-essential-oil)

Sounds like a spell. There is a certain enchantment as you walk into a house or room where these essential oils are infusing. It has a way of captivating your senses so that you are carried away on a wisp of emotions. Please understand, I am not trying to be mean, but ladies love that sort of thing. The "magical" trip of your mind and emotions carried away to a mental world of artificial reality. A fake and lying world of emotion. It's like magic!

Perhaps you say, "Well, what's wrong with that?" What's wrong is that it lusts against the Holy Ghost of God, it's witchcraft, and it is sin.

Ah yes, doTerra! Ah yes, YoungLiving! Many of the "Christian" ladies in the churches I am around are using these brands. Yes, some men use them as well, but the vast majority is women.

Hope, by **By Faith Oils**

Bring encouragement to the heart and feel your spirits lifted with this pleasant smelling blend, extremely helpful for depression and other times when life can bring you down.

(https://www.byfaithoils.org/collections/synergy-blends/products/rejoice-blend-aromatherapy-pure-essential-oil)

With this blend, nothing has changed, except you feel better and encouraged. The oil blend made you feel better. Your life is not any better, your situation is not any better, and as a matter of fact, by using this blend you made the situation worse. How? Because now that you "feel" better, you will not "feel' the need to pray to the Lord Jesus Christ, and you will not "feel" the need to claim some of the promises of God found in the word of God. No, but now that you have breathed in these scents, you "feel better" but you're not any better. You actually are worse. The "feeling" you acquired from the infused oils is a lie!

> **44 Ye are of your father the devil,
> and the lusts of your father ye will do.
> He was a murderer from the beginning,
> and abode not in the truth, because
> there is no truth in him. When he
> speaketh a lie, he speaketh of his own:
> for he is a liar, and the father of it.
> (John 8)**

This second blend, which used to be called "Rejoice" but is now called "Hope" is produced and sold by a "Faith" based company. By Faith Oils is a non-profit company where, "all proceeds go to Christian charities."

Now, I am not trying to be mean or ugly, and I am sure they are sincere, love the Lord and so on, but they are wrong!

The Lord Jesus Christ said:

> **2 They shall put you out of the
> synagogues: yea, the time cometh, that
> whosoever killeth you will think that
> he doeth God service. (John 16)**

History is filled with graveyards from people who thought they were serving God when according to the word of God, they were deceived by the Devil.

Uzza thought he was doing right when he stretched out his hand to steady the ark and God killed him. Eve was beguiled and thought that she was doing good, when she was sinning against God. David was loving God and trying to please God when he brought the ark back to Jerusalem, but he carried it on a Philistine cart and that attempt turned to tragedy. On the second attempt he had the ark carried according to the scriptures and God blessed him.

What am I saying? I am saying that it is very easy to be deceived about things and the only remedy for deception is the truth.

17 Sanctify them through thy truth, thy word is truth. (John 17)

Whether a company is Christian or not does not determine whether what they are doing is Biblical or not. There are many faith based companies and ministries selling essential oils that claim to be serving the Lord Jesus Christ. What they fail to realize is that they are beguiled. They think that they are doing good, but in reality, they are missionaries for Satan. So was I.

When my wife was supposedly "healed" of her allergy to milk I began to proclaim it on the internet, as well as in the churches that the Lord Jesus Christ had answered prayer and healed my wife of her allergy to milk. When I began to proclaim this, I became a missionary for Satan. The Holistic remedy that we used is contrary to the word of God, though at the time we did not realize this. Fortunately within five weeks we realized it was wrong and repented. Guess what. The moment we repented, Terri's milk allergies returned. It showed us that she was never really healed. You are dealing with an unclean spirit. You are practicing witchcraft!

My main point about this is that the King James Bible of 1611 states in the book of Galatians, which is written to Christians, that witchcraft is a work of the flesh. What that means is that witchcraft is a work of the flesh. Did it say, "Witchcraft?" Yes, it said, "Witchcraft!" Or should I say, "It READS, Witchcraft."

There are other "Bible-based" Christian companies just like this. Here are some others: Selahessentialoils.com, Edensgarden.com, and hopewelloils.com .

Listing these companies seems frivolous to me, since many of the Christians that I know who are using essential oils are purchasing other brands. The main brands they use are doTerra, Young Living and Nature's Sunshine. Some of these may have associations with "Religion," but the bottom line is whether you purchase essential oils from a Christian-based company, a secular-based company, or a Witchcraft-based company, *the product of essential oils is all the same.*

Not only that, but the use of the oils is all the same as well. In the generic sense (no pun intended) the following is true whether you purchase them from Christian, secular, or a witchcraft supply company.

1. All three sell essential oils
2. All three specify the requirement of natural and not synthetic oils.
3. All three declare synthetic oils have no power
4. All three sell infusers for the infusing of the oils
5. All three promote aromatherapy for healing
6. All three promote essential oils for the same purposes, the same methods, with the same supposed results.

Both Christian and secular suppliers sell their oils and aromatherapy products to support and improve health and wellness. These are the exact same reasons witchcraft suppliers market their essential oils, and those reasons are included in the works of witchcraft. Just go to the websites and examine them for yourself. What I have just written is not hard to verify, if you want the truth.

As a matter of fact, notice the following: By Faith Oils is a massage therapy clinic.

> We are a professional aromatherapy / massage therapy clinic...
> (https://www.byfaithoils.org)

I'm not just making this stuff up. More important than the companies that sell essential oils is the fact that Christians are doing what the witches do, the same way, and for the same reasons.

I will be listing three types of companies.

1. Those who sell essential oils among other things for the practice of witchcraft.

2. I will also list companies who sell essential oils, among other things, but who profess a faith/Bible based philosophy.

3. And lastly, I will list secular companies that sell essential oils among other things.

Along with each listing I will include what each recommends and the descriptions for the use of the essential oils. Though not exactly the same wording, (nothing in Witchcraft is exact for they claim it's an individual journey. One where you are in charge. I am not trying to be mean, but the problem is that at the end of your journey is a lake of fire. Rev. 20:15) yet the works performed by witches and those in the metaphysical activities are identical to those performed by the other two groups, faith and secular.

All three groups are using, and they must be, natural pure essential oils, infused into the air for the purpose of health and healing. The healing may be emotional, or physical, or spiritual, but they (all three), use the essential oils for the same thing, the same way, and for the same reasons.

Yes, Witches have a broader listed range of "workings." Notice the activities of witches are called workings. The point is that the Faith-based descriptions have much in common with occult-based witchcraft. According to the word of God in Galatians 5, they are one and the same.

The act of warming, or infusing spirits (essential oils), into the air for the purpose effecting the person's body, whether mind, flesh or spirit, are one and the same. The Christians are doing the works of witchcraft, and in so doing they are committing spiritual adultery. The Bible calls it witchcraft, and it is against the Holy Ghost of God. It grieves Him. It quenches Him. It defiles your person and greatly hinders the Holy Ghost from working in your life.

On top of that it will remove your inheritance in the millennium so that you will not reign with Christ for 1000 years. Notice, "...they which do such things shall not inherit the kingdom of God." Yes, you are still saved and going to Heaven, but you will lose your inheritance. Your salvation is not inherited, your salvation is a gift from God.

> **8 For by grace are ye saved through faith; and that not of yourselves: it is the gift of God: 9 Not of works, lest any man should boast. (Ephesians 2)**

Briefly, your inheritance has to do with you reigning with Jesus Christ for 1000 years on this earth with the Lord Jesus Christ. (Rev. 20, Rom 8:17, Col. 3:24, 2 Tim. 2:12). It is said to be a reward in Colossians 3:24. Rewards can be earned, and rewards can be lost. The prodigal son came home, but no longer had an inheritance. (Luke 15:31). The thought of walking around on this earth for 1000 years in shame is not something that I would really trifle with. The tears are not wiped away until after the millenium. You need to stop and think about that!

Practicing witchcraft will remove your inheritance, unless you repent and judge yourself. The Bible states, "...if we would judge ourselves, we should not be judged." (1 Cor. 11:31) You can get things right here and now, but if you continue on in sin you will regret it. After all, we are talking about witchcraft. Notice the terms used to describe the effects of various essential oils.

There are some terms that are used by each online store in the descriptions of what these essential oils are used for. If you are like me, I did not know what some of the terms meant, so I am going to define some of the terminologies here so you will know what they mean. The following terms are used in the practice of witchcraft. I looked the words up in a few dictionaries, but as you will see, they didn't have the proper definitions for the words. I had to go to websites that are dedicated to witchcraft in order to get the definitions that applied to the use of these oils.

The Bible is such an accurate book! This is so sad, but think about the following. Even the

"Christian" or "Faith Based" Essential oils stores use terms that are part of the every day terminology in witchcraft. So, now you have "Christians," pastor's wives, deacon's wives, and dedicated church members using the terminology that is used by witches in the practice of witchcraft.

The first word to define is the word, "Centering."
American Heritage Dictionary
Centering: cen·ter·ing (sĕn'tər-ĭng) n.

A temporary, usually wooden framework on which an arch, vault, or dome is supported during construction. (American Heritage® Dictionary of the English Language, Fifth Edition. Copyright © 2016 by Houghton Mifflin Harcourt Publishing Company. Published by Houghton Mifflin Harcourt Publishing Company. All rights reserved.)

Somehow, I just don't think the use of the word "Centering," in the context of essential oils, has anything to do with the temporary wooden framework upon which an arch, vault, or dome is supported. I just don't think that would apply to essential oils.

Here it is again:
Oxford Dictionary:

1. The action or process of placing something in the middle of something else.

Example Sentences
'Once this is done, with appropriate hacks for Internet Explorer (which does not implement minimum and maximum heights), vertical centering is achieved.'

- 'The horizontal centering is not a problem.'
- 'I love the intensity of a whirlpool's centering of things.'

(https://en.oxforddictionaries.com/definition/centering)

Somehow, though, it just doesn't seem like this definition from the Oxford Dictionary is correct either. I doubt that essential oils have any effect upon Internet Explorer or the operation of a whirlpool.

But since essential oils are used by witches, maybe if I look to witchcraft for the definition I'll be able to get some understanding about the activity of Centering.

Witchipedia
Centering is an energetic practice. When we center ourselves we gather our energy, which may be scattered in many different places, and we harness it toward our intention.

Centering is an important skill that is

often taught early on to students of magick because it allows us to be fully present in our magickal workings, reducing the likelihood that they will be contaminated by outside energies and concerns, thereby increasing their effectiveness and safety. Magickal techniques for centering vary.

(http://www.witchipedia.com/def:centering)

Well, how about that! Eureka! I go to a website about witchcraft and get a definition that fits with the use of essential oils. Perhaps the reason is because it is witchcraft. Perhaps these "Christians" that are using essential oils are practicing witchcraft.

Centering, Balancing, Grounding, and Shielding are terms in witchcraft that have to do with "energy." In aromatherapy these terms are not used for the control of your emotions and mood. They are terms that have to do with the spirit energy, or Qi of your body, or the Qi of the place in which you are currently located. They are terms used in the practice of witchcraft, and Christians are now using those terms and performing the works associated with those terms. If that is you, dear reader, then you are practicing witchcraft, and you are grieving the Holy Spirit.

Christians are notorious for re-labeling sin. Adultery is now called "stepping out." Drunkeness is now called "substance abuse." Witchcraft is now called "holistic healing." The word of God calls it sin!

Centering is often combined with the term "Grounding."

Grounding

> **Merriam-Webster** - Definition of grounding: training or instruction in the fundamentals of a field of knowledge.
>
> (https://www.merriam-webster.com/diction-ary/grounding)

> **Cambridge University:**
> Grounding: a knowledge of the basic facts about a particular subject:
> Example: This course is designed to give drivers a grounding in car maintenance.
> (https://dictionary.cambridge.org/us/dictionary/english/grounding)

Once again, somehow, I just don't think this has anything to do with the use of essential oils. If I could gain knowledge by sniffing something it would sure be easier to go to school and get good grades. I sure would have loved to have something to sniff when I was in Algebra. (I hated Algebra). The people that I have known over the years that have sniffed things, really didn't gain any knowledge. As a matter of fact, it seemed to burn out their brain and the lining of their nose.

No, I don't think this definition for Grounding will work with essential oils. It must have to do with something else. Once again, I think I will try to find the definition in the realm of witchcraft. Perhaps that is the place to find the definition for the word "Grounding." Well, let's see what the witches have to say about grounding.

Here is the definition of "Grounding" from: witchipedia.com

> Grounding is the process of connecting with and becoming aware of our physical body and its connection with the Earth. It allows us to siphon excess (nervous) energy into the Earth while allowing us access to the limitless energy of the Earth. Grounding has the effect of settling the mind and body and allowing the practitioner better focus and is considered by many to be a foundational spiritual activity.
>
> As a daily meditative practice, grounding is said to improve and maintain health; physical, mental and emotional.
>
> As a part of magickal practice,

grounding assists in the direction and maintenance of the flow of energy while reducing the stress upon the channel or practitioner.

Grounding may also be called Earthing. Earthing is a term more commonly used among the New Age and alternative healing community. Grounding is the term used most often by magickal practitioners, though I expect there are geographical differences in the terminology. (http://www.witchipedia.com/def:grounding)

A Christian friend of mine told me of how he was practicing Karate and his instructor told him that he needed to ground himself. Finally he focused his feet mentally to the floor. When he did this something happened, that seemed to glue his feet to the floor. He told me that he was now able to throw someone, or flip someone and all the while, it was as if his feet were glued to the floor. By doing that he had leverage from which to fight. The problem was the energy of the grounding is against the word of God. You are talking about Qi, AKA Chi, Ki or Prana. It is an unclean spirit.

Unfortunately the following story is of a pastor that I had known. He was an excellent Bible teacher and preacher and I had the privilege of sitting under his ministry and teaching. At the time I was under his ministry he did not do what I am going to describe for you here. As a matter of fact, he taught against it and called it occult.

The fact of him practicing and using witchcraft goes to show that, as the Bible proclaims, "...all **flesh is grass.**" (Isa. 40:6) We are all sinners, and as the old song says, "Prone to wander, Lord I feel it. Prone to leave the God I love."

The seriousness of the following true story is the fact that this Bible teacher was practicing witchcraft in the last years of his life. He was so deceived, that he would demonstrate Qi manipulation in Bible class, church, as well as in other churches when he was a guest preacher. He justified his actions because he was beguiled into thinking that it was merely his spirit that he was working.

There have been three or four occasions where someone had told me about being in one of his classes and he would call a couple strong men up to the platform. He would place each man on either side of him and ask them to take him by the arm and pick him up. Being the small man that he was, they could easily pick him up. Then this teacher would "focus his Qi and ground himself." After focusing his Qi he would ask each man to take him by the arm on each side and lift him off the platform. They could not pick him up off the floor.

I had another man tell me the same thing. He had attended a "revival" meeting at a church in North

Carolina where this man was going to be preaching. With a large congregation present, this Bible teacher called two male volunteers up to the platform to demonstrate his centering. He held his arms out flat and then focused his Qi. He then told the men to try to pull his arms down, and they could not.

The man that told me the story was one of the men that volunteered. He stood on one side, with another man on the other side and he personally told me that he could not pull his arm down. This Bible preacher had centered himself metaphysically so that his arms stayed out stretched. Sad, very sad indeed!!!

If that is such an "innocent" thing, then why did Moses need Aaron and Hur to hold his arms up?

The last term I want to define is the word, or term "Shielding." What is Shielding?

It is important to remember that when descriptions are given for definitions of workings in the context of witchcraft, that they are talking about *energy*. The heart of witchcraft is the raising of energy, and then directing it to accomplish the will of the one directing it. This "energy" originates from Satan, for he is the prince of the power of the air. King James so aptly describes the witches in his book Daemonolgy as, "slaves of the Devil".

(Daemonologie, King James, Book 1, page 5, Sacredtexts.com)

In the workings of witchcraft and the use of this "energy" which is nothing more than spirit, is the fear that negative energy will come back upon them. Of course I am describing the actual workings of witches. Among the holistic crowd of healers are similar fears, especially in Yoga when they are dealing with serpent power which is also known as Kundalini. There are many stories of people having very bad experiences with Kundalini. Many precautions are prescribed for those beginning to work with Kundalini.

So in regards to "negative energy" there is what's termed "shielding." This is where a person puts up a shield or force field to protect them from negative energy. Again, I did not know this when I started this study. In the descriptions of essential oils I would see the words, "shielding, protection, purification, and cleansing."

For the average person, these descriptions can be confusing. Often times I see this in the descriptions for the uses of essential oils. Cleansing or purification is taken by Christians to mean house cleaning and sterilization of the environment, but that is not the true meaning of the words in the context of aromatherapy witchcraft. Cleansing and purification has to do with clearing out unwanted energies.

So here is another word that I want to define within the context of aromatherapy witchcraft. Whether you intend to use the oils this way is irrelevant, for this is the true definition for the use of these oils.

What does the word shielding mean? As with

Aromatherapy

Grounding and Centering, let's first look in a regular dictionary to find the definition of the word.

Merriam-Webster online only has the word, "shield" - a broad piece of defensive armor carried on the arm.

No that won't apply to shielding with essential oils.

> Collins has a definition that is a little better - 1. countable noun
>
> Something or someone which is a shield against a particular danger or risk provides protection from it.
>
> (https://www.collinsdictionary.com/us/dictionary/english/shield)

Again, this does not fit with the use of essential oils. So let's see what is the definition from a source in the realm of witchcraft.

> Wicca.com - Let's start with Shielding. This is a technique for creating a magical 'force field' around your person or a place, to keep out unwanted energy.
>
> (https://wicca.com/celtic/wicca/defense.htm)

There you go. That will fit for the uses of essential oils. If you see a description for the use of an essential oil, or blend of oils, and you see the word shield, shielding, purification, or protection, it has to do with energetically putting a force field around you to block out unwanted energies, or clearing out unwanted energies and protecting you from their returning.

What do witches use, among other things for shielding? They use essential oils to perform this work of witchcraft.

For example here is:

Joellessacredgrove.com -

Juniper Berry essential oils, "The Essential oil is useful in protection."

(http://www.joellessacredgrove.com/Herbs/g hijk-herbs.html)

Youngliving:Sacred Mountain

Essential oil - Sacred Mountain™ is a blend of Ylang Ylang and conifer oils that evokes the sense of sanctity found in nature and promotes feelings of strength, empowerment, grounding, and protection when diffused. (https://www.youngliving.com/en_US/products /sacred-mountain-essential-oil)

Empower Your Oils:

...it's essentially magic - Podcast - The Oil of Shielding - Today's pod is all about the oil of Shielding. We are talking about the empowerment of doTERRA TerraShield essential oil blend:

Strengthens the protective shield around one's body, helping them to feel safe***

Teaches individuals to hold strong boundaries and not allow themselves to be pushed around***

(https://www.empoweryouroils.com/single-post/2017/06/02/The-Oil-of-Shielding)

In the psyche of a witch, they must shield themselves by putting up a force field around themselves to protect them from unwanted and negative energies. I am so glad that I am saved!!!

Essential Oil Supply Companies Compared

A description of each company and the link to each company is listed in the Bibliography of this book.

There are three catagories compared:
1. Witchcraft Supply Store for Essential oils
2. Faith Based Supply Store for Essential oils
3. Secular Supply Store for Essential oils

Things to notice about the charts
1. Faith based is almost identical to the Witchcraft based oil descriptions. This would be

expected since witchcraft is a work of the flesh.

2. Purification and cleansing are virtually identical descriptions

3. Healing used in all but one cell in the charts.

Aromatherapy

Witchcraft Isisbooks:	**Cypress** **Essential Oil**	Grief
Witchcraft 13 moons:	**Cypress** **Essential Oil**	Healing,Comfort, Balancing, Protection
Witchcraft Joellesacredgrove Magical uses	**Cypress** **Essential Oil**	Healing, Grief, Protection
Witchcraft Witches of the Craft:	**Cypress** **Essential Oil**	Protection, uplift at funeral/grief
Faith Based ByFaithOils	**Cypress** **Essential Oil**	Medicine, Soothing to the mind ie. Grief: my comment
Faith Based Selah Essential Oils	**Cypress** **Essential Oil**	Healing, Grief, Depression
Faith Based Eden's Garden	**Cypress** **Essential Oil**	Healing, Anti-Septic, Respiratory
Faith Based Hope Well Oils	**Cypress** **Essential Oil**	Anxiety, Healing, Nerves
Secular doTerra	**Cypress** **Essential Oil**	Grounding in times of loss, Vitality, Energy,
Secular Young Living	**Cypress** **Essential Oil**	Grounding, Security
Secular NOW	**Cypress** **Essential Oil**	Balancing, Clarifying, Centering
Secular Natures Sunshine	**Cypress** **Essential Oil**	Grounding, Peace, Skin Care

Witchcraft Isisbooks:	Eucalyptus	Health, Purification
Witchcraft 13 moons:	Eucalyptus	Healing, Protection, Purification
Witchcraft Joellesacredgrove Magical uses	Eucalyptus	Healing, Purification, Protection
Witchcraft Witches of the Craft:	Eucalyptus	Purification and Healing
Faith Based ByFaithOils	Eucalyptus	Healing, Decongestant
Faith Based Selah Essential Oils	Eucalyptus	Healing, Decongestant
Faith Based Eden's Garden	Eucalyptus	Purifying, Decongestant, Respiratory
Faith Based Hope Well Oils	Eucalyptus	Respiratory, Healing, Mental Focus
Secular doTerra	Eucalyptus	Decongestant, Purification, Calming
Secular Young Living	Eucalyptus	Cleansing, Calming
Secular NOW	Eucalyptus	Revitalizing, invigorating, clarifying
Secular Natures Sunshine	Eucalyptus	cooling soothing, changing of the seasons

Aromatherapy

Witchcraft **Isisbooks:**	Frankincense	success, spirituality
Witchcraft **13 moons:** Magical uses	Frankincense	spirituality, protection, depression, grounding, meditation
Witchcraft **Joellesacredgrove** Magical uses	Frankincense	Healing, Meditation, spirituality, love, protection
Witchcraft **Eclectic Artisans**	Frankincense	aiding spirituality and magic
Faith Based ByFaithOils	Frankincense	Skin care, Decongestant, Meditation, Sacred uses, Calming
Faith Based Selah Essential Oils	Frankincense	Healing, Calming, Depression
Faith Based **Eden's Garden**	Frankincense	Anointing oil, Meditation, Healing, Calming
Faith Based **Hope Well Oils**	Frankincense	Healing, Calming, Mental Fatigue, Stress (Is Uplifting)
Secular **doTerra**	Frankincense	Healing, skin, calming, relaxation, balance mood
Secular **Young Living**	Frankincense	Spirituality, meditation
Secular **NOW**	Frankincense	Relaxing, Focusing, Centering
Secular **Natures Sunshine**	Frankincense	Centering, Meditation Prayer

104

Witchcraft Isisbooks:	Juniper	Healing, Protection
Witchcraft 13 moons:	Juniper	Love, health, Purification, Male Potency
Witchcraft Joellesacredgrove Magical uses	Juniper	Love, Protection, Healing blends, Male Potency
Witchcraft Alchemy Woks	Juniper	Purification, Clairvoyance, Protection
Faith Based ByFaithOils	Juniper	Cleansing, health, healing
Faith Based Selah Essential Oils	Juniper	Calming, Healing, Depression, Prostate, Antimicrobial,
Faith Based Eden's Garden	Juniper	Calming, Strengthening
Faith Based Hope Well Oils	Juniper	Healing, Calming, Prostate, Purify
Secular doTerra	Juniper	Detoxifying, Cleansing, Grounding, Calming, Healing
Secular Young Living	Juniper	Peaceful atmosphere, Self Confidence, Purifying
Secular NOW	Juniper	Restoring, Empowering, Balancing
Secular Plant Therapy	Juniper	Calming, Meditation, Purification

Aromatherapy

Witchcraft Isisbooks:	Lavender	Success, Communication, Memory
Witchcraft 13 moons:	Lavender Sleep, Love,	Purification, Happiness, Healing, Calming, Balancing
Witchcraft Joellesacredgrove Magical uses	Lavender Sleep, Peace, Joy, Healing,	Attracts Elves (Yes, you read that right), Balancing, Love
Witchcraft Eclectic Artisans	Lavender	Cleansing, Healing, Love
Faith Based ByFaithOils	Lavender	Healing, Calming, Antimicrobial, Antitoxic
Faith Based Selah Essential Oils	Lavender	Calming, Sleep, Cleansing, Anxiety, Depression
Faith Based Eden's Garden	Lavender	Calming, Balance, Restoration
Faith Based Hope Well Oils	Lavender	Balancing, Calming, Stamina, Energy, Skin
Secular doTerra	Lavender	Calming, Sleep
Secular Young Living	Lavender	Skin care, Calming, Soothing, Balancing
Secular NOW	Lavender	Soothing, Normalizing, Balancing
Secular Natures Sunshine	Lavender	Sleep, calm, Relaxation

106

Witchcraft Isisbooks:	Lemon	Protection, Energy
Witchcraft 13 moons:	Lemon	Purification, Love, Cleansing, Energizing
Witchcraft Joellesacredgrove Magical uses	Lemon	Healing, Purification
Witchcraft Eclectic Artisans	Lemon	Healing spells, love, energy, boost healing energies
Faith Based ByFaithOils	Lemon Uplifting, Cleansing, Antibacterial	Concentration, Memory, Immune system, Circulation
Faith Based Selah Essential Oils	Lemon Cleansing, Circulation-stimulating	Antifungal, antimicrobial, antibacterial, Mental alertness
Faith Based Eden's Garden	Lemon	Cleansing, Uplifting
Faith Based Hope Well Oils	Lemon	Cleansing, Energizing, immune support
Secular doTerra:Top Selling oil	Lemon Cleansing, Purifying, Invigorating	Digestion, Uplifting, Energizing, Positive Mood
Secular Young Living	Lemon	Cleansing, Skin, Hair, Cheerful
Secular NOW	Lemon	refreshing, Cheerful, Uplifting
Secular Natures Sunshine	Lemon	Stimulating, elevate Mood, Cleansing

Aromatherapy

Witchcraft	Cypress	Healing, Grief/Comfort, Protection
Faith Based	Cypress	Healing, Grief, Soothing to the mind
Secular	Cypress	"Grief", Security/Protection, Skin/Healing
Witchcraft	Eucalyptus	Healing, Purification
Faith Based	Eucalyptus	Healing, Purification
Secular	Eucalyptus	Purification Cleansing
Witchcraft	Frankincense	Healing, Meditation, uplifting Depression
Faith Based	Frankincense	Healing, Meditation, uplifting Depression
Secular	Frankincense	Healing, Meditation, Centering

Witchcraft	Juniper	Healing, Male Potency, Purification
Faith Based	Juniper	Healing, Prostate, Cleansing
Secular	Juniper	Healing, Cleansing Purifying
Witchcraft	Lavender	Healing, Sleep, Balancing, Calming
Faith Based	Lavender	Healing, Sleep, Balancing, Calming
Secular	Lavender	Healing/Skin Care, Sleep, Balancing, Calming
Witchcraft	Lemon	Healing, Cleansing/Purification, Energizing
Faith Based	Lemon	Healing/Immune Support/Circulation, Energizing
Secular	Lemon	Healing/Digestion Skin, Cleansing, Uplifting/Cheerful

Aromatherapy

Chapter 5

Dangers Of Using
Essential Oils

The vast majority of the time Aromatherapy and its use of essential oils are touted as safe. After all, goes the proclamation, they're natural, they must be safe! Beware! The assumption that they are safe because they are natural is not true, for essential oils are chemicals that have been refined from plants. The ingredients of essential oils amount to hundreds of chemicals.

(Punctuation errors are preserved from the original)

Despite mammoth scientific and technological advancement, modern science can still not unlock the secrets of essential oils Chemical components that nature combines to make up the oils, could not be replicated till date. Even after identifying hundreds of constituent chemicals, mixing those constituents in right proportion and with the best human efforts, one would still not have an identical oil. Such a copy of an oil will not found to have the same impact as the natural and pure essential oil. It may be due to the reason that an essential oil has more than several hundred components, and figure may run up to thousands; many of them may not be detected or identified so far. As such, it is not possible to say about the definitive number of compounds an essential oil can contain.

(Dr. Yogesh Chandra Tripathi Ph.D./Forest Research Institute Dehradun FRI · Division of Chemistry and Bioprospecting - https://www.researchgate.net/post/What_is_the_maximum_number_of_compounds_an_essential_oil_can_contain)

Notice he says that they are chemicals. Sure, all of nature is chemicals, molecules and such, but essential oils are refined substances from their original materials. Yes, I said refined. To refine,

Webster 1913 definition: "1. To reduce to a fine, unmixed, or pure state; to free from impurities; to free from dross or alloy; to separate from extraneous matter; to purify; to defecate; as, to refine gold or silver; to refine iron; to refine wine or sugar."

So essential oils are a refined substance that consists of hundreds of chemicals! They are not natural, for in their natural organic state dispersed among the materials, they contain impurities. Essential oils are refined from the extraneous matter because there is not enough concentration for them to accomplish anything when left in their organic natural state.

So when you hear someone claim that essential oils are in the Bible, they don't know what they are talking about. The materials that contain essential oils such as frankincense and myrrh are in the physical state which is not desired nor used by those who promote aromatherapy.

Incense is mentioned in the Bible, so in a way, aromatherapy is in the Bible, but not in the form that is popular today. Frankincense is obviously incense as stated in its name.

Another interesting fact is that essential oils are not essential. What I mean is that the name implies for them to be essential, but that is not the origin of their name. Their name comes from the word essence. As I have already stated the quint essence is a spiritual energy known as Qi. For the naive populace it is proclaimed that essential oils are an attempt to capture the essence, or scent of the material from which it is refined. Many of them

113

do strongly carry that scent, to that there is no doubt. By claiming they are merely capturing the essence or scent, it subtly camouflages the true occult nature of essential oils.

So now, these chemicals that are being infused into the air, rubbed on the skin, or even taken orally, can bring about problems that are rarely talked about and even hidden when they are mentioned.

I have had people tell me that they were having nightmares all the while they were using essential oils. Yes, the essential oils were causing nightmares, for the nightmares stopped when they repented, and stopped using the essential oils.

I had a newly married Christian lady tell me the following story. She had never used essential oils. But she had not been feeling well, so a friend of hers, who sold essential oils came over and treated her in order to help her get better. Part of the treatment was to apply essential oils to the feet. I am not sure what else was done at the time. Probably, just my guess, a blend was infused into the air.

From that point on she began to experience panic attacks, which was something she had not experienced before. Confused as to what was happening, she would call her father and he would read the Bible to her over the phone. Then he would pray with her until the panic attack went away. This went on for a few weeks.

My wife and I came over to see her, not knowing

114

what was happening. She then told us of the problem and we asked if she had begun or changed anything in her house or life. She told us that she had been treated with the essential oils and even had some in the house to use, which had been given to her from her friend.

We explained the danger of the use of essential oils, and told her that at the core of their use, it is witchcraft and a sin against the Lord Jesus Christ. We told her that the use of essential oils opens a door to the occult world and allows an unclean spirit to enter into and afflict you.

That night after we left, she and her husband knelt in prayer, and repented of using the essential oils. They cleaned all of it out of their house and guess what? The panic attacks stopped.

I know another young girl who was treated by a pastor and his wife who were using essential oils, as well as reflexology and acupuncture. She had never experienced panic attacks before, but after her visit she began to have panic attacks as well. Unfortunately, at that time we did not know the danger of using the essential oils, as well as the other works, so we did not know how to counsel her. I do not know if she still suffers from the panic attacks or not.

I know a man who wrote a book on essential oils and he told me the following story:

There is a family in his church that has a teenage girl. Through their mother, they were introduced to aromatherapy and the use of essential oils. Not long after their using of the oils the daughter began to have nightmares and thoughts of suicide. That's right suicide! It completely shocked them as to why she would be going through such a horrible battle.

It got so bad that she was of afraid of sleeping in her bedroom. Out of fear she would go into the parents bedroom and sleep on the floor. In spite of this, things kept getting worse. The nightmares got worse, to the point she was afraid to go to sleep. She began to realize the trouble started around the time the essential oils were brought into the house. Because of this realization, she did not want to be in a room if it had the essential oils in it.

Finally, the mother and father believed her, and realized that her problems began after they started using the essential oils. They subsequently cleaned them all out of the house, and her nightmares and suicidal thoughts went away. This is not a game! You are messing with witchcraft!

What I am about to say, you need to seriously think about. If you are a born again Christian, then the powers of darkness do not like you. If they can use you to mess up other Christians, then they may allow you to carry on with little to no problems. However, if the unclean spirits can not use you for their purpose, then they can enter through the door that you have opened, and ruin your life, health, family, and testimony.

Kurt Koch was a Christian author who studied

and wrote much about the occult. In his book Occult ABC he writes about a Christian young man who went to an iridologist for diagnosis and healing. (An iridologist is someone who claims to diagnose sickness by reading the iris of the human eye. In witchcraft, it is termed oculomancy which is a form of divination).

This young man recovered of his sickness, but soon after he noticed some very troubling changes. He would have severe pain when he started to enter a church. Along with this he would have pain and discomfort if he tried to read his Bible or pray. Then he became depressed, began to abuse drugs, and eventually had a nervous breakdown. The unclean spirit that he used for "healing" came to steal, kill and destroy, which it did.

Prepubertal Gynecomastia

Here is some of the latest information on one of the dangers of essential oils and aromatherapy. It is a risk to do this, for many people have no interest in the true scientific evidence when it comes to things like this. As David Hill, (who is an advocate for the use of essential oils) the chief medical officer of doTerra, and who had been the director of Gary Young's Utah Clinic, has said:

> But the conclusions reached by scientists are beside the point for many

117

consumers. 'I'll use my wife as an example,' Hill said. "She's not going to be able to tell you the first thing about chemistry. Put a research paper in front of her—zero interest. And that's probably how most people are. What's real to them is the experience they're having.

(https://www.newyorker.com/magazine/2017 /10/09/how-essential-oils-became-the-cure-for-our-age-of-anxiety Rachael Monroe)

The Bible puts it this way.

> 3 For the time will come when they will not endure sound doctrine; but after their own lusts shall they heap to themselves teachers, having itching ears; 4 And they shall turn away their ears from the truth, and shall be turned unto fables. (2 Timothy 4)

I realize that we are in the time when people are turning their ears away from the truth and turning to fables. But hopefully you are not one of them! The truth is that essential oils and Aromatherapy is science, falsely so called, which we are warned against.

20 O Timothy, keep that which is committed to thy trust, avoiding profane and vain babblings, and oppositions of science falsely so called... (1 Timothy 6)

If you don't have a King James Bible then you will miss the "Heads up" in regards to subjects like this one that is the topic of this book. The word "science" has been removed from the modern versions of the Bible. Even the New King James Version has removed the word "science." The Bible warning is to avoid falsely called science.

For years when I read this verse I automatically thought of Darwin's theory of evolution. After realizing the truth about New Age Medicine, or Holistic Medicine, I realized that it is false science. They try to make it sound scientific, which it is not!

If you go into, (and I would not recommend this), the office of a naturopath, iridologist, acupuncturist, or to an office that practices reflexology, or aromatherapy, you are going to find charts, explanations, and supposed evidence for the veracity of the use of the holistic treatment that you are getting ready to use. Contrast that with a dentist office, or a general practitioner of medicine.

In a real doctor's office, they do not spend a lot of time trying to explain or convince you of the merits of the treatment he/she believes is necessary for your health or healing. They do not try to prove to you that it is scientific, safe, or natural. When the doctor diagnoses a patient, he may give a brief explanation of the problem and why he is prescribing the specific medicine. Generally speaking, in a real doctor's office, they have nothing to prove. They are real doctors, prescribing real medicine, as well as performing legitamate medical procedures.

Aromatherapy is not scientific! Yes, you read that right. The scientific basis for Aromatherapy is not there. Factual scientific evidence is not essential for "touchy feely" people who will proclaim, "I just know what I feel." It is more important to go by what the word of God says, than what one feels. To claim you are proceeding by feeling is characteristic of a strictly emotional mentality. Feelings are unpredictable and changeable. The truth is unchangeable and solid. To proceed by feelings is to build upon shifting sand. When the winds come and the rains descend, the Bible states,

26 And every one that heareth these sayings of mine, and doeth them not, shall be likened unto a foolish man, which built his house upon the sand: 27 And the rain descended, and the floods came, and the winds blew, and beat upon that house; and it fell: and great was the fall of it. (Matthew 7)

You had better make sure you are building upon the solid foundation of the truth or you are going to end up in a mess. Aromatherapy does not have true science on its side.

There has been some true scientific evidence come out in 2018, that is associated with the use of essential oils. Before I cover it, I am going to back up to 2007, to another study that was done at Ohio State University.

The following information was taken from Ohio State News

Columbus, Ohio - Aromatherapy May Make You Feel Good, But It Won't Make You Well.

"One of the most comprehensive investigations done to date on aromatherapy failed to show any improvement in either immune status, wound healing or pain control among people exposed to two often-touted scents." "In some cases, even distilled water showed a more positive effect than lavender." (The two scents they used to evaluate were lemon and lavender essential oils.)

(https://news.osu.edu/aromatherapy-may-make-you-feel-good-but-it-wont-make-you-well---030308)

Aromatherapy

Do you care about these true scientific findings? Does it matter to you? Or are you just going to go by your feelings? So many users of aromatherapy respond with, "Well, I know what I have seen." Pragmatism is not, I repeat, *is not* the basis on which to establish you actions. You must remember that Satan is the master of deception.

> **22 For false Christs and false prophets shall rise, and shall shew signs and wonders, to seduce, if it were possible, even the elect. (Mark 13)**

The following study was published online in the Journal of Psychoneuroendocrinology:

> In this study, Dr. Ronald Glaser, Professor of molecular virology, immunology and medical genetics, along with Dr. Janice Kiecolt-Glaser, Professor of Psychiatry, and Dr. William Malarkey Professor of internal medicine, "looked for evidence that such aromas go beyond increasing pleasure and actually have a positive medical impact on a person's health. While a massive commercial industry has embraced this notion in recent decades, **little, if any, scientific proof**

has been offered supporting the products' health claims." (Emphasis added). "We all know that the placebo effect can have a very strong impact on a person's health but beyond that, we wanted to see if these aromatic essential oils actually improved human health in some measurable way."

"While lemon oil showed a clear mood enhancement, lavender oil did not, the researchers said. Neither smell had any positive impact on any of the biochemical markers for stress, pain control or wound healing... We still failed to find any quantitative indication that these oils provide any **physiological** effect for people in general."

(http://www.elsevier.com/wps/find/journaldescrip tion.cws_home/473/description#description)

What that means is beyond affecting your mood, aromatherapy does not have an effect physically, on the body.

"We measured a lot of complex physiological interactions instead of just a single marker, and still we saw no positive effect."

This is according to Ohio State University

The following is from Yale Scientific, the nation's oldest college science publication, by Cynthia Deng, 1/16/2011.

Aromatherapy: Exploring Olfaction.

"While there may be evidence for aromatherapy's mood altering effects, scientific proof for physiological improvements is lacking. Most of the evidence for reducing pain and decreasing healing times is anecdotal rather than scientifically grounded. In fact, a recent study at Ohio State University found that aromatherapy did not cause any physiological effects. While lemon oil did improve moods, neither lemon oil nor lavender significantly changed pain ratings, heart rate, blood pressure, wound healing, or stress hormone levels. The lack of physiological response to lemon oil and lavender, two of the most popular scents, seems to indicate that aromatherapy does not provide all the health benefits that spas and other essential oil businesses often claim."

(http://www.yalescientific.org/2011/11/aromatherapy-exploring-olfaction/)

Not only is the scientific evidence lacking for the positive physiological effects of essential oils, there is scientific evidence that essential oils can have **negative physiological effects on young boys.**

A report in the Journal of Pediatric Endocrinology and Metabolism, 2015-09-03, Volume 29, Issue 1, mentions three young boys "who presented with prepubertal gynecomastia and were chronically exposed to lavender. Two of these boys were exposed to a cologne, named aqua de violets, used by Hispanic communities in the US, and in their countries." Conclusion: Exposure to estrogenic substances, such as lavender, should be explored in children presenting with prepubertal gynecomastia/thelarche."

(https://doi.org/10.1515/jpem-2015-0248)

What they found was the young boys, due to the exposure to lavender (it did not say what form the lavender was other than for two of the boys, it was cologne) **were growing female breasts, or should I say the boys' breast were developing similar to the way young girls' breasts develop. Not only did the lavender mimic estrogen hormone in the body of the young boys, but it also hindered the**

125

production of testosterone, the male hormone.

In another study there were three other boys who presented with the same symptoms. This was reported in the:

New England Journal of Medicine 2/01/2007.

"On the basis of the three case reports and the in vitro studies, we suspect that repeated topical application of over-the-counter products containing lavender oil or tea tree oil was the cause of gynecomastia in the three patients... The results of our in vitro studies indicate a dose–response relationship in the estrogenic and antiandrogenic activities of lavender oil and tea tree oil... "

(N Engl J Med 2007; 356:479- 485 DOI:10.1056/NEJMoa064725,https://www.nejm. org/doi/full/10.1056/NEJMoa064725)

The following report in the New England Journal of Medicine had the same findings as the 2015 report in Journal of Pediatric Endocrinology and Metabolism. These findings added more evidence that lavender and tea tree oils not only mimic estrogen and cause young boys to grow female breasts, but they also block the production of testosterone in the young boys.

Now, in March of 2018 there was the annual meeting of the Endocrine Society in Chicago. Endocrine has to do with the endocrine gland:

Definition - Endocrine glands release (secrete) hormones into the bloodstream. (U.S. National Library of Medicine - https://medlineplus.gov/ency/article/002351.htm)

The research team (J. Tyler Ramsey, B.S., Yin Li, PhD, Yukitomo Arao, PhD, and Kenneth Korach, Ph.D.) took four chemicals that appear in both lavender and tea tree oils (eucalyptol, 4-terpineol, dipentene/limonene and alpha-terpineol) and four that appear in either oil (linalyl acetate, linalool, alpha-terpinene and gamma-terpinene)... Of note, according to Ramsey, these chemicals are not specific to lavender and tea tree oils and appear in 65 other types of essential oils as well. The research team found that these chemicals may act like estrogens and block androgens like testosterone in ways that could give boys bigger breasts. (https://www.forbes.com/sites/brucelee/2018/03/18/will-essential-oils-like-lavender-and-tea-tree-make-your-breasts-larger/#4795fbc03fc2)

Perhaps this explains why we have more and more young boys wondering if they are a girl or not? If they grow up in a home where essential oils are flooded through the air, or slathered on the body, then according to multiple scientific, repeatable studies, the essential oils that include the chemicals (yeah, real natural!) eucalyptol, 4-terpineol, dipentene/limonene and alpha-terpineol, as well as linalyl acetate, linalool, alpha-terpinene and gamma-terpinene, will mimic the production of estrogen, the female hormone. They will also block the production of male androgen hormones among which is testosterone. Those young boys will become effeminate. Now we know the reason many boys think they are girls.

In reference to this report Dani Stringer is quoted in Healthline:

> Dani Stringer, MSN, CPNP, PMHS, a pediatric nurse practitioner from Arizona, agreed that parents should know about the possible harms of essential oil. "Too often I encounter patients that wrongly consider essential oils to be natural and therefore automatically believe that they are safe. This is not the case," Stringer told Healthline. "The high concentration found in essential oils can definitely impact the body and this

is seen even more in children. Now we are discovering the hormonal impact they can have as well."

(https://www.healthline.com/health-news/ essential-oils-hormone-disruption-for-boys#1)

As for the ability of lavender essential oil to effect female hormonal levels notice the following quote from Dr. Kurt Schnaubelt, who is an advocate for the use of essential oils:

> Essential oils of *Vitus agnus cactus* is today used by many in the aromatherapy community as a highly effective and safe agent to equilibrate progesterone and estrogen levels, significantly easing PMS and menopausal complaints.
>
> (The Healing Intelligence of Essential Oils, Kurt Schnaubelt, Healing Arts Press, 2011, pg 86)

So you now have multiple documented cases where young boys are growing breasts like girls when they are exposed to essential oils, at the very least, topically. Though lavender, as well as 66 other essential oils, have not been tested for the efficacy upon young boys by infusing them into the air, would you want to risk having your son around them?

Aromatherapy

This is extremely instructive since it is common that couples who begin to use aromatherapy end up with a strong female dominating the house with the husband becoming passive and reserved. Again, this is to be expected in that witchcraft will bring about results that are opposite of what the word of God commands.

> **23 For the husband is the head of the wife... (Ephesians 5)**

> **1 Likewise, ye wives, be in subjection to your own husbands;...4 even the ornament of a meek and quiet spirit, which is in the sight of God of great price. (1 Peter 3)**

> In the book, Magical Recipes by Dr. R. N. Ashley, one can find an oil recipe called Mistress of the House Oil. This magical potion is unknowingly placed in "hubby's" shoes and will allow the wife to wear the "pants" in the family. (At The Crossroads - An Essential Truth, Jim Spivey, 1652 Hedrick Mill Rd. Lexington, NC 27292)

In the witchcraft community, and due to the fact that the vast majority of witches are female, there are many such recipes and spells to enable the women to control the house. The problem is that when they do, they are not happy with that either.

Now, I need to get back on topic of this chapter, which is the dangers of essential oils. They are commonly considered safe because they are "natural." No, they are not natural, and often are very dangerous.

According to the Ohio State University study, they could produce no physiological benefits as to healing. However, there are negative physiological effects when it comes to hormonal production in young male boys who have been the subjects of topical application of essential oils.

In my opinion, from personal observation, I have watched marriages change when the wife using essential oils shows a change in personality. She becomes dominant, and the husband, has a change in personality as well, and becomes passive. This would strongly suggest that the testosterone production has declined, or stopped.

Another danger with certain essential oils is the fact that expeller pressed citrus oils are photocarcenogenic. This means that if a person applies non-distilled essential oils to their skin, and then goes out in the sun it can cause cancer. It seems I can almost hear someone proclaim, "Oh, but they are safe and natural."

There have been people who have ingested essential oils and burned their throat as well as their stomach.

A very real danger is for someone who is legitimately sick with cancer, and instead of seeking true medical help, they go to the naturopath aromatherapist for healing and end up dead. By the time they wake and realize that they should try the real medicine it is too late and they die.

A sad story:

She was a vibrant energetic pastor's wife that the ladies of the church loved greatly. One day she was diagnosed with breast cancer. Going to a proper medical doctor she allowed them to operate and remove the tumor. After the surgery she healed well and went back for a post operative check up.

The doctor told her that she would need another regimen of chemotherapy as the type of cancer that she had was known to return. With the chemotherpy, they had extremely good chances of survival, getting healed, and going on to living a normal healthy life.

After seeing her natural doctor she opted for holistic therapy, instead of the medical doctor's recommended therapy. Upon returning for a check up the doctor told her again, that she needed to do the regimen of chemo, but she refused. The doctor was very upset at this and told her plainly that with the chemo she would very likely recover and live a normal, healthy life. She refused and he made her sign a form stating that she was refusing his advice.

She used the holistic medicine treatment, and after a certain amount of time, the cancer returned.

132

She did not seek her doctor's help for quite awhile. Though doing the holistic treatments, she continued to grow weaker and sicker. Finally she decided to go back to her doctor for help.

There in the doctor's office he said to her, "I cannot help you now. It's too late, and you have waited too long to come to me for help. I told you we could have dealt with this months ago, and you would have been fine, but now it is too late. I'm sorry, I cannot help you." Not long after that she died.

Stories like this happen over and over to people who have listened to fake medicine, also known as witchcraft.

10 The thief cometh not, but for to steal, and to kill, and to destroy: I am come that they might have life, and that they might have it more abundantly. (John 10)

Wendy's Story

The following personal testimony was sent to me. I know the author and this is her story in her own words.

My brother, sister and I, (all single adults) were living together at the time. A very sweet, Christian

133

lady whom we had come to know introduced us to essential oils when we came down with colds. After setting up our new air infuser we began using some oils she had given us.

At the time a friend had shared some concerns with us about them being connected to witchcraft. Their information was pretty vague, so we asked around and tried finding out more about essential oils. We found the whole thing to be perplexing to us. When we looked online we found that witches did indeed use them, but we also knew good Christian people who used them, as well. We wondered if maybe it was more of an issue of "how" they were used? Reasoning with ourselves, but still doubtful, we figured they were all natural therefore they must be safe, right? We did not know what to think.

After discussing it further with our parents we decided to pray about it and let the Lord show us if there was something wrong with using them, and to make it clear to us if we should not be using them.

Over the next few weeks we began experiencing some really odd things going on around the house. Some were more obvious than others, and some we didn't "put together" 'til days later, that anything was amiss. Strange, random things like when our sewing machine showed up on the table. We do a lot of sewing at our house. My sister and I each have our own sewing machine. So we didn't really think anything of it. I thought it strange but assumed my sister had used my machine, and she assumed I had done some sewing on my machine. But a few days later when something was said about it we discovered that neither of us had. We even asked our brother if for some odd reason he had pulled it out. But nobody in our house had it out or used it at all that week.

Another strange thing was when I came home to find that the cap to my perfume bottle was off and sitting next to the bottle. On any day of the week that would have caught my eye because I very habitually put it back on after using it, so it literally was one of the first things that I noticed as I stepped into my room. But what was even crazier was the cap that was sitting next to the perfume bottle, did not even belong to it. I had never seen this cap before. The original cap was no where to be found, and the one that was there fit it, but clearly did not belong to it. It was a different color and had leopard spots on it. I have never even owned anything with leopard spots on it. This was extremely puzzling to me and really creeped me out.

One evening my sister was sitting on the couch and heard noises in the kitchen behind her like dishes clanging in the sink. Thinking it was me, she turned around to say something only to find that nobody was there.

On another day, my brother came home from

work ahead of us girls. My sister and I worked at a greenhouse so he knew we'd be out that day. He jumped in the shower as usual and when he was done saw that the lights were on down the hall and thought to himself, "Looks like the girls got home". Without coming out he flopped on the bed for a nap before supper. A bit later he came out and found the lights off and us girls no where to be found. Thinking it odd that we would leave without saying anything he gave us a call to see where we were. We apologized for being late and explained that we thought we'd run some errands since we were already in town and would be heading home soon.

"You mean you never came home? " he queried, "I was sure you were here". We assured him we weren't. "That is crazy!", he exclaimed. "I got out of the shower and the lights were on, and I was sure I heard you out there, too. I laid down, and when I got up the lights were off!" We scratched our heads...it seemed like we were all going a little crazy lately.

During this same time I noticed that some of my decorations on top of the fridge were shuffled around. It was as though someone had been in the cabinets behind there. Another mystery as nobody claimed responsibility for doing anything up there.

The real "clincher" though, was the bright, sunny day that I came into the house and sat down on the couch only to discover that it was wet. "What on

136

earth?" I got up and examined it. Sure enough, a large wet spot covering most of the cushion. With a bit of grumbling, I thought to myself, "That brother of mine! I bet he dozed off and spilled his drink again! He could of at least put down a towel so someone would know it was wet." When my brother came in I mentioned it to him. He looked at me puzzled, "What!? I didn't spill anything."

And so, all around the mulberry bush went the questions once again. "Are you sure?" "You're absolutely positive?" " Nobody spilled anything here!? " The three of us stood there looking at it. This was the craziest thing ever. Our roof did not leak, and it hadn't rained in days anyway; we did not have any indoor pets to blame it on. There was absolutely no explanation for it. Water does NOT just appear on couches by itself out of the thin air! By this point I was pretty flipped out. And it was then that it dawned on me - could any of this be related to the essential oils?

We began to recap all the odd, unexplained things that had been happening in the past few weeks. The sewing machine, my perfume bottle, the lights, the noises, the stuff on top of the fridge, what was really going on here? Were we in some way opening ourselves up to some kind of demonic activity by using and having these essential oils in our home?

We tried to think of every reasonable explanation possible. Could someone be breaking into our house? But if so, it was strange that they were only coming in to use our sewing machine, exchange perfume lids, rummage through kitchen cabinets, and dump water on our couch! Nothing in the house of any value was missing. It just didn't make sense. When did all this stuff start happening? We pulled out the calendar and recalled every detail we could. As best as we could figure it all began just after we started using the essential oils. We decided it just seemed too coincidental. We collected the oils, took them outside and burned them. After we burned them we didn't have any more crazy things happen and everything was back to normal.

Chapter 6

The Flesh Lusts
Against The Spirit

Preface of this chapter

Aromatherapy and the use of essential oils will not be the primary subject of this chapter. This chapter will deal with motives and secondary issues that surround Aromatherapy. I debated with myself whether or not to include this chapter. Was it relevant enough to include this information or not? Obviously, I decided it was. I hope to explain and communicate the seriousness of the subject. In a way, to me this is one of the most important aspects of this subject and speaks to the heart of the matter.

I may get "preachy" at times in this chapter. I make no apology for it. This is not a game. This concerns the grieving of the Holy Spirit of God. It is not to be taken lightly.

THE BATTLE

> 16 This I say then, Walk in the Spirit, and ye shall not fulfill the lust of the flesh. 17 For the flesh lusteth against the Spirit, and the Spirit against the flesh: and these are contrary the one to the other: so that ye cannot do the things that ye would. (Galatians 5)

The flesh, which is your body, is contrary to the Holy Spirit of God. In a very real sense, they are opposites. The flesh is corrupt, but the Holy Spirit is Holy, pure and good. The flesh is temporary, but the Holy Spirit is eternal. The flesh is sinful, but the Holy Spirit is Holy and righteous. The flesh enjoys sin, but the Holy Spirit hates sin and never sins. The flesh lusts against the Holy Spirit, and the Holy Spirit lusts against the flesh.

In the book of Ephesians, there is a similar battle mentioned, but it is mentioned as the old man and the new man. Some of you reading this already understand this battle. Some of you do not, and for those who do not understand this battle, I am going to give you a brief explanation of it.

If you do not understand what the Bible says about the old man and the new man, you may begin to doubt your salvation. Likewise if you don't understand the battle between the flesh and the

140

Spirit, then you can get to the point of believing that if you commit these works of the flesh, then you have lost your salvation or that you were never saved.

Can a Christian commit any of the sins in this list and still be saved? Yes! Galatians and Ephesians are both written to Christians. Will you lose your salvation if you commit these sins? No! Will you reap what you sow? Most definitely! Not only in this life, but at the Judgement seat of Christ, as well as in the millennium. You will lose your inheritance.

How can a Christian take part in witchcraft and be saved? Or how can a Christian commit adultery and be saved? This is not hard to answer, if you understand and believe the word of God.

> **22 That ye put off concerning the former conversation the old man, which is corrupt according to the deceitful lusts; 23 And be renewed in the spirit of your mind; 24 And that ye put on the new man, which after God is created in righteousness and true holiness. (Ephesians 4)**

Did you notice in those verses that it said, "ye put off," and "ye put on?" These are commands that a saved child of God is to do. Even after you are saved, you still have a free will. Both the old man and the

141

new man have desires, but you cast the deciding vote as to which one you are going to give in to.

We had been traveling all day. The fuel was getting low, so we stopped at a truck stop to fill up, use the restroom, and get a bite to eat. Night had fallen and thus it was dark outside. The truck stop had the parking lot lit up like it was day time, which was good since it was a rough area.

We walked out to our truck, and as I was getting ready to climb into the cab of the medium duty International, a security guard was standing on the sidewalk, not too far away from me. He looked to be in deep thought, but the kind of thought showed as somewhat painful upon his face.

I struck up a polite simple conversation and asked him, "How are you doing tonight?" He didn't answer quickly, but after a slight delay he responded, "Oh, I'm doin' alright...I guess."

I continued, "If you don't mind me asking', if you died tonight do you know for sure that you would go to Heaven?"

This got his attention. He turned his head and looked at me with the reply, "I don't know."

I then asked him if he had ever asked the Lord Jesus Christ to forgive him of his sins, and to come into his heart and save him?"

To this he replied, "Yes, I have done that. It was a couple years ago."

He gave some more particulars about when he got saved, and it was to the point that I was sure he

142

had been born again. The problem was, he wasn't sure he was saved. In the course of the conversation he told me that he was having bad thoughts. He was married, but things weren't going as smooth as he would want. He and his wife were not at the point of divorce, but they were having problems finding the right time to be husband and wife.

He then said, "If I am saved, then why am I having all these bad thoughts. Thoughts that I shouldn't have." I told him that he had an old man and a new man. The old man was the one thinking those thoughts.

"When you were lost you had those thoughts, right?" I asked him.

"Oh yeah! I had these thoughts." He replied.

Back then, these thoughts didn't bother you did they?

"Nope, not at all." He said.

I then said, "But now they do, don't they?"

He hung his head and said, "Yeah, they do."

I then said, "That's because you are saved. It bothers you now, when before it didn't."

His eyes widened, he looked at me and said, "You're right! It didn't use to bother me, but now it does."

We continued on in our conversation with me showing him the battle and why he was having it. Little by little his assurance of salvation was growing and he was getting more settled in his

143

emotions. I prayed with him and left.

If you do not understand that there is a part of you that is not regenerated, then you will not understand why you still have the thoughts and temptations that you do. The old man does not want to do right. Even though you are born again, there is still a part of you that rebels against God. There is in you, that is your flesh, a rebelliousness that if you were at Calvary the day Jesus Christ was crucified, you would be crying out, Crucify Him, Crucify Him!" That rebellion is in you, and it is in me right now.

Even though you are saved, why do you still want to do wrong? Because you are still in this old rotten flesh. This old rotten, corrupt flesh does not want to do right.

If you are born again, there is inside of you a new man that is created in righteousness and true holiness. That new man wants to do right. It wants to read the word of God, pray, and do those things that are pleasing in His sight. Remember, however, that you also have a free will, and the one you choose to obey depends upon your love for God, at that given moment.

Let me give you an example of what I am talking about.

Let's say you are sitting in front of your computer with no one else around. You pull up the internet and begin to surf the web. Perhaps you go to youtube. There in front of you are video clips of various subjects. Many of those videos go against the word of God, and others do not.

You see the title of one clip and the flesh, the old man, says, "That looks good. Wouldn't that be fun to watch!" But then another impression comes and says, "That is not right! You know you shouldn't look at stuff like that."

Now you have a decision to make. You may give into the old man and click, but then change your mind and submit to the new man. That battle may jump back and forth three or four times, from the old man to the new man and back. You know that you shouldn't watch certain things, yet a part of you wants to watch them. That battle, you are going to have for the rest of your earthly life, but one day you are going to get a new body. It will be a glorified body that will always do right. That is going to be a glorious day!

NO MIDDLE GROUND

In the list of the works of the flesh that is given in Galatians 5, let me ask you some questions. The first work of the flesh that is given is adultery. Is adultery an issue where Christians will separate over? Yes, it is! Well, it used to be. Is there any middle ground when it comes to the work of adultery? No there isn't! Sex with someone, other than your spouse, is sin. This work of the flesh is worth dividing over.

145

> 4 Marriage is honourable in all, and the bed undefiled: but whoremongers and adulterers God will judge.
> (Hebrews 13)

Is there middle ground with the work of fornication? No!

> 19 Now the works of the flesh are manifest, which are these; Adultery, fornication, uncleanness, lasciviousness, 20 Idolatry, witchcraft, hatred, variance, emulations, wrath, strife, seditions, heresies, 21 Envyings, murders, drunkenness, revellings, and such like... (Galatians 5)

This list of works are contrary to God; there is no middle ground. If you are on the side of God, then there is no middle ground when it comes to this list. If you are saved and give into the flesh, knowingly or unknowingly, then when it is brought to your attention that you have committed any one of these acts, there ought to be a repenting and confession of sin to the Lord Jesus Christ. You don't confess these acts of sin to a man, but to the Lord Jesus Christ and He is faithful and just to forgive you your sin and to cleanse you from all unrighteousness.

If you make excuses, or try to justify your sins,

then you are not right with God. If a church, pastor or saint, seeks to make alibis for the commission of these sins and thus allow them to continue in the church fellowship of believers, then that church is not right with God. It will fall down the slippery slope into apostacy. There is no middle ground with regard to these things. These works of the flesh are contrary to the Holy Spirit!

A church that will allow adultery, or not deal with adultery in the membership of the congregation will become a spiritually dead church. The exact same thing may be said for all of these works! If they are allowed to take place in a church, that church is grieving the Holy Spirit and the services will become very dead and dry.

If these things fail to be judged and corrected by the leadership of the church, then the church will spiritually die. When not dealt with, and not preached against, the leadership of the church will usually take a course of action that has nothing to do with God and everything to do with money. They will prop up the services with a manufactured fake excitement that is based upon music. A substitute for the Spirit of God will be brought in and it will be centered around music. The rationale will be for souls and to "relate" to the new generation. Sadley, the reality is that the Holy Spirit will have left many months earlier.

30 And grieve not the holy Spirit of God, whereby ye are sealed unto the day of redemption. (Ephesians 4)

147

When you give into your flesh, it grieves the Holy Spirit, who is in your body. Not only is the Holy Spirit in your body, but Jesus Christ is in your body as well.

> **27 To whom God would make known what is the riches of the glory of this mystery among the Gentiles; which is Christ in you, the hope of glory...** (Colossians 1)

When you give into the flesh, and in particular for this study, when you use witchcraft, then you grieve your Saviour, the Lord Jesus Christ as well. The mere thought of that ought to bother you.

INTENTION

If the use of essential oils and Aromatherapy is witchcraft, and it is, then you are grieving the Holy Spirit as well as your Saviour. You are sinning against the Holy Ghost of God when you do what the witches do when they practice witchcraft. It has nothing to do with your intention! It has everything to do with what you are doing, not why you are doing it. Jesus said the time will come when **"whosoever killeth you will think that he doeth God service."** (John 16:2) You had better judge by what the Bible says, and not by your

148

deceptive heart.

For me, this is the heart of this book. Is Aromatherapy and the use of essential oils right or wrong? That is one very important question that needs to be answered. To me, there is another more important question which is, "Does the use of Aromatherapy and essential oils grieve the Holy Ghost, as well as the Lord Jesus Christ?"

If something I am doing grieves my Saviour, then I do not want to do it! If I do, (for I am still living in my wicked sinful body of flesh), then I must confess my sin to Him, knowing that He is faithful and just to forgive me my sin and to cleanse me from all unrighteousness.

Does the thought of hurting your Saviour bother you? It should! Does the thought of grieving the Holy Spirit bother you? It should! If it doesn't I wonder if you are saved? Have you ever been truly born again? The word of God states that the works of the flesh are contrary to the Holy Spirit of God, and as such they quench and grieve Him. I don't want to do that, do you?

There are people mentioned in the Bible that thought they were doing right when they were doing wrong. There are people in the Bible that thought they were helping God or doing something pleasing to God, when they were actually sinning against Him! The Bible term, or word for that is "beguiled", and it is what happened to Eve.

The Bible states that the woman being deceived

was in the transgression. The point is not that she was a woman, but that she was deceived. She thought that she was doing a good thing when in reality she was sinning against God.

You may proclaim, no! She knew exactly what she was doing, and chose to go against God anyway. Well, she did go against God, to that there is no doubt, but the Bible states, **"...the serpent beguiled Eve through his subtilty."** (2 Cor. 11:3)

In the book of Joshua chapter 9, Joshua, the leader of Israel was beguiled. Joshua and the nation of Israel met a group of people who appeared to be from a far country. Their clothes were dirty and ragged. Their shoes were worn out, and their food was old and moldy.

Now, God had told Joshua and the nation of Israel, that they were to wipe out the nations when they came into the promised land. The only ones they could not destroy were the cities that stood still and did not fight back. Those they would save alive.

> **13 But as for the cities that stood still in their strength, Israel burned none of them, save Hazor only; that did Joshua burn. (Joshua 11)**

Israel was commanded to destroy the the rest of the cities and nations.

The Gibeonites did not know the part about

standing still. They were fearing for their lives, so they decided to make a deal and get Israel to swear before God that they would not destroy them, which they did. Somehow the Gibeonites knew that if the Israelites would sware before God that they would not hurt them. Israel's oath bound them before God and they had to keep their oath.

> 1 And Joshua made peace with them, and made a league with them, to let them live: and the princes of the congregation sware unto them. (Joshua 9)

Once Joshua and the princes swore, then they could not go back on their word, for then would God punish them.

As Israel journeyed, three days later they came to the cities of Gibeon and realized what they had done, so that they could not destroy those cities. Then Joshua said this to the Gibeonites,

> 22 And Joshua called for them, and he spake unto them, saying, Wherefore have ye beguiled us, saying, We are very far from you; when ye dwell among us? (Joshua 9)

Joshua "thought" that he was doing right, when in actuality, he was doing wrong and disobeying

God's command to Israel.

The Bible states that Eve was beguiled, and even Eve admits this:

> 13 And the LORD God said unto the woman, What is this that thou hast done? And the woman said, The serpent beguiled me, and I did eat. (Genesis 3)

She still suffered the penalty of disobedience and so did Joshua and Israel, but what I want you to see is that at the time of the commission of the sin, they thought that they were doing right. They were beguiled.

Have you ever been beguiled? You thought that you were doing right, and some time after the Holy Spirit revealed to you that you had sinned against God.

> 23 For the commandment is a lamp; and the law is light; and reproofs of instruction are the way of life... (Proverbs 6)

This age is a time where it is very easy to get into sin. With the electronic devices as they are, just a mere click and you can be immersed into a world of sin. Additionally, there are times when you have done something sinful and have not even known it

152

because the Christians around you were doing it as well. Perhaps it was a common activity practiced amongst those whom you admired and respected, but now the Holy Spirit, through the word of God has revealed to you that it is sin.

We had started out in evangelism and things were going very well. Along the way we had the privilege to meet people and make new friends. And they became very close friends that are dear to our hearts.

One pastor I went hiking with, brought along his "medicine chest" which was a little wooden box with homeopathic "remedies" in it. When he pulled it out and I saw it, I thought it was "cool." That's the California in me, and I looked upon the medicine chest with favor. This pastor, a man that I looked up to and admired, loved the Lord, and was doing a great job in the ministry. I never once at that time thought there was anything wrong with that little chest of "natural medicine!"

Another time I had a pastor's wife treat me with more homeopathic "remedies" for my voice. I was losing my voice and she was genuinely trying to help me. She even purchased a large bottle of homeopathic medicine that I am sure cost quite a bit of money. Again, I never even considered anything was wrong.

In another church, the pastor's wife pulled out her little box of essential oils, anointed my feet and started rubbing them according the the various zones of reflexology. (My wife was present). All the while, I never dreamed that what she was doing was against the word of God...but it was!

Another pastor's wife paid for Terri and I to go to a naturopath that she used. Again, it was an attempt to help my voice, which was progressively getting worse and worse. The naturopath muscle tested me, diagnosed me using iridology, and prescribed supplements for treatment. For my voice, it had absolutely no effect or help, but again, I also never for a minute thought anything was wrong, or that I had grieved the Holy Spirit. Obviously, my walk with the Lord was not close enough that I could tell any difference.

Another time, Terri was treated with Nimbudiprad's Allergy Elimination Treatment (N.A.E.T.) At the time she was "healed" of her allergy to milk, but thankfully, in just about one month we realized that something was wrong. After hearing a testimony about muscle testing, and the dangers of New Age Medicine, we repented broken hearted and contrite. Upon confessing our sins together, and then separately we got our hearts right with God.

The works that we got into, and which were against the word of God we became involved in because there were good people that we trusted, looked up to, and to a certain extent, followed without question.

In this age in which we live, it is very very easy

to end up in sin. Upon the realization, it can shock you because often sin appears so "good or innocent". Then it breaks your heart because you know you have sinned against your Saviour. You did not realize was sin. You were beguiled!

This sinful period is termed by some, as the time of Laodicea from Revelation 3. I agree with that. It is the Laodicean time in which we live, and it is very sinful, carnal, and covetous. There is a verse in that portion of scripture that you need to observe which is this.

19 As many as I love, I rebuke and chasten: be zealous therefore, and repent. (Revelation 3)

If you want God to continue to deal with you, then you must be willing to repent when He shows you sin in your life. If you are not willing, obedient, and repentent when he convicts you, then little by little He will let you go your own way.

This brings up a question. How long has it been since you were under conviction? How long has it been since you were convicted by the Holy Spirit, repented and confessed it to the Lord Jesus Christ? How long has it been since you were convicted about something that you had never seen before? You are supposed to be growing in the Lord, right? Well, if you are growing in the Lord then there will be things that the Lord reveals to you that you did not see two years ago. Don't compare yourself to those you hang around with, but apply the word of God to your heart and life.

If it has been years since you were under conviction that ought to trouble you greatly! I have not arrived yet, and neither have you! Yes, there are sins that I am aware of and I confess them daily, just as there are sins with you that you ought to confess daily to the Lord in prayer. Carefully consider, when was the last time you were under conviction, repented and confessed it to God? If it has been a while, perhaps He has let you go your own way, or worst yet, perhaps you are beguiled and think you are pleasing the Lord Jesus Christ, when actually you are sinning against Him.

Perhaps you ask, "How do you know?" You know by reading the Holy words of God daily and praying over them daily, asking God to deal with you in whatever way He knows you need.

> 23 Search me, O God, and know my
> heart: try me, and know my thoughts:
> 24 And see if there be any wicked way
> in me, and lead me in the way
> everlasting. (Psalms 139)

Let me give you a challenge, and it is not something that I don't do myself. I pray often for the Lord Jesus Christ to search me, and know my heart; to try me, and know my thoughts. Lord, please see if there be any wicked way in me, and lead me in the way everlasting.

I pray that often. So I am asking you. Will you pray over this book? Will you ask the Lord Jesus Christ if what I have written is true or false, based upon the Word of God rightly divided? Not based upon your feelings, or the opinions of your friends.

It's just you and Jesus Christ. Will you surrender to whatever the Lord shows you through His word? Not through me, but compare what I have written with what the word of God says, and pray over it. Do you want to please God? Is it possible for you and me to be beguiled? Of course it is! The only tool to destroy error is truth, the inerrant word of God, which is the 1611 King James Bible.

Aromatherapy

Chapter 7

Substitutes For Spirituality

After a couple of hours working on this book, I had taken a short break. Upon return to my desk I sat down to write some more, but my mind was distracted. I bowed my head, closed my eyes, began to pray and ask my Saviour, Jesus Christ, to help me concentrate and to proceed with writing.

I had been studying the definitions of Centering, Grounding, and Balancing. Each one of those words are significant in the practice of witchcraft, but they are also mentioned in the therapeutic purposes of the essential oils. In both instances the words are being used to describe the same workings. Whether it is witchcraft supply stores, faith-based "Christian" supply stores, or secular supply stores, these three words are all used identically, but I did not know what they meant, so I searched for a definition of each.

The specific information that I was trying to

organize and write down were the definitions to the acts of Centering and Grounding. I had just read a number of articles on those two acts and had obtained a good understanding of there meaning. As a matter of fact, as I was praying and asking the Lord to reign in my thoughts and to help me concentrate, I realized that what I was doing was similar to the definitions of Centering and Grounding, specifically the centering.

For a split second I almost prayed and asked the Lord Jesus Christ to help me Center and Ground myself. What?!?! Are you kidding? These two thoughts exploded in my mind. Then I easily caught myself in my conversation with the Lord Jesus Christ and praying out loud said that, "I would never ask you to help me perform acts of witchcraft."

The Biblical prayer is to ask the Lord to help you, to reign in your thoughts, to help you cast down your imaginations, and to help you think on those things that the Lord wants you to think on.

> 8 Finally, brethren, whatsoever things are true, whatsoever things are honest, whatsoever things are just, whatsoever things are pure, whatsoever things are lovely, whatsoever things are of good report; if there be any virtue, and if there be any praise, think on these things. (Phillipians 4)

In witchcraft practices of Centering and Grounding, SELF becomes the object of your thoughts and mind. In those definitions given earlier of centering and grounding, self is the object of the activities.

That is completely against the word of God for, **"Thou wilt keep him in perfect peace, whose mind is stayed on thee."** (Isaiah 26:3) It is typical for witchcraft to put your mind upon yourself. All of witchcraft can be summed up in this statement, "my will be done."

This is totally contrary to the word of God, for your mind is not to be focused upon yourself. Your mind is to be stayed upon the Lord Jesus Christ. I know that is easier said than done. I do not profess to have accomplished that. But for certain you are not to practice placing your thoughts upon your body or yourself. The result of doing so will make you self centered, which is the opposite of what the word of God says you ought to be. This is typical for witchcraft! At the root of it all is rebellion which is, "My will be done."

I thought, as I prayed, what a fool I would be if, instead of going to my Saviour in prayer for help and strength, I inhaled some essential oils instead. That would be the beginning of my falling away from Jesus Christ. What's more is that I would be grieving the Lord as well.

Jesus Christ stated that, **"Without me ye can do nothing."** (John 15:5) That is what your Creator said, and He knows what He is talking about. You can use all of the essential oils you want, but it will only take you into a downward spiral. Instead of drawing nigh to Jesus Christ, you are substituting a whiff of essential oils instead. That is bad...very bad!

A Substitute for true spirituality

The Natural medicine crowd constantly assails the western medical community for popping pills. The accusations immediately fly when the subject comes up that all they do is tell you to pop a pill and you will be fine. According to the Holistic crowd, western medicine is merely treating the symptoms and not the true cause of the disease, or problem, which is a lie. Yes, it is a lie. They then proclaim that their natural medicine, and the holistic treatments treat the cause and not merely the symptoms. This is also a lie.

Do you know what happens to the majority of people who seek holistic remedies to fight heart disease? They drop dead! Do you know what happens to people who seek holistic treatments to fight severe Pneumonia? They drop dead! Do you know what happens to people who seek holistic treatment for a bad hip? They use a wheel chair!

I get so sick and tired of the lies being espoused from the realms of witchcraft. When Hudson Taylor went to China the natives lined up to be treated by

162

a real doctor. Why? Because their medicine was wounding and killing them.

I talked to a missionary who works in China teaching the English language to the Chinese people. She said in her class were young girls with scars on their necks from cupping and moxibustion. Moxibustion is where they stick an incense cone on the skin by rubbing milk on the bottom of the cone to make it stick to the skin. They then light the incense cone and let it burn all they way down to the skin, and it stays on the skin until it burns out. It causes severe blistering and scarring to the body of the poor patient. It is all a bunch of sick superstition, and the devils are laughing themselves silly watching the pain and suffering take place. In my book Defiled, I mention a missionary to China who said the devils always liked it when the people would harm themselves.

Holistic medicine does not treat the cause. For one, all the holistic crowd can treat is the symptoms because, in the United States they cannot legally practice true medicine. But the real lie that comes from the imaginations of these deluded souls being influenced by devils is this. If I have heard it once, I have heard it a thousand times, and they could not be any more wrong. The cause of "dis-ease" is a lack of homeostasis. In other words, you need your energies balanced. Yin and Yang are out of balance. The innate intelligence is blocked by a subluxation. Kundalini is not rising properly. Or your mind, body, and spirit being are not functioning as one. All those workings are Science falsely so called (1 Tim. 6:20) according to the word of God, and it is designed by the god of this world, to bring you into bondage.

Back to my original thought, which is, instead of the western medicine's prescribing of pills, the holistic crowd reaches for a whiff of essential oils. You can see them all over the place. Dabbing and rubbing scents on their body all day long. They often appear agitated, psychotic and can't relax. They're driven by their concern for themselves, constantly trying to decide which oil will "cure" their current symptom.

Others have to stay mindful of their meridian clock, so they know which meridians are in focus at any given time of the day. All of this "natural" medicine puts a person in bondage; it does not liberate. It also places your mind upon yourself and definitely not upon the Lord Jesus Christ where it ought to be. Oh, but it sounds so good doesn't it?

Here is an aromatherapy blend called, "Peace."

doTerra - Use the **doTERRA Peace** Reassuring Blend to promote feelings of contentment, composure, and reassurance when anxious feelings overwhelm your emotions.

(https://www.doterra.com/US/en/p/peace-re-assuring-blend-oil)

YoungLiving - Peace and Calming - Diffuse this oil to freshen the air, especially in rooms where children play or study.

Apply to the bottom of feet before bed as part of a bedtime ritual for your whole family.

(https://www.youngliving.com/en_US/products/c/essential-oil-products/blends)

ByFaithOils - Tranquility -

Our most popular synergy blend: A comforting blend that encourages calm and rest. Tranquility is soothing and peaceful to promote quality, restorative sleep.

(https://www.byfaithoils.org/collections/synergy-blends)

13moons - witchcraft supply - Stress Relief blend - Relieve stress by using in bath: 6 - 8 drops; as a body rub/massage oil; or place on cotton ball or tissue and inhale.

(https://www.13moons.com/shop-by category/essential-oils/oil-blends)

No, of course you don't believe in popping pills, but you will reach for some witchcraft remedy and grieve the Holy Ghost of God in a heart beat. God's way of obtaining peace, tranquility, and relief for stress is by praying and standing on the promises of the word of God.

> 7 Casting all your care upon him, for he careth for you. (1 Peter 5)

> 28 Come unto me, all ye that labour and are heavy laden, and I will give you rest. (Matthew 11)

> 22 But the fruit of the Spirit is love, joy, peace... (Galatians 5)

Do you want peace? Do you need peace in your life? Then you need to repent of your sins and get filled with the Holy Spirit! If you will get your heart right with God, then you will have peace, but you certainly will not get peace by sniffing scents, rubbing oils and using witchcraft. The Bible says that, **"the just shall live by faith."** Physical applications of physical things in order to obtain spiritual qualities are not of faith, and whatsoever is not of faith, is SIN!!!

Instead of going to the Lord Jesus Christ, you have a knee jerk reaction and run to your essential oil witchcraft for emotional stability. The fleeting momentary pleasure soon evaporates and the emotional instability soon returns. The difference now is that you have sinned against God, so now you are going to be convicted by the Holy Spirit of your sin. The unpleasant "feeling" from the

166

conviction, you mistake for an imbalance in your homeostasis.

Again you seek relief through your oils, but now you are fighting the one who is convicting you of sin. You are now fighting God and it is a downward slippery slide to weakness, sickness and eventually death.

> **30 For this cause many are weak and sickly among you, and many sleep. (1Corinthians 11)**

You have an idol, and you are believing a lie, which is blocking you from going to your Saviour.

Why, it's to the point where people, mostly women, have jewelry with Essential oils in it so they wear it all day long. But the Bible says that, **"Whatsoever is not of faith is sin."** Many of you are to the point where you are overcome with fear if you don't have oils on your body all day long. You are in bondage, and it is not of God.

doTerra - Essential oil blend - **Console:** The doTERRA Console Comforting Blend uses sweet floral and tree essential oils to promote feelings of comfort, putting you on a hopeful path of emotional healing.

(https://www.doterra.com/US/en/pl/proprietary-blends)

ByFaithoils - **Anxiety** - When you need a little extra comfort and peace add into your life the calming effects of this essential oil blend. Designed exclusively for times of high anxiety and stress.

(https://www.byfaithoils.org/collections/synergy-blends)

EdensGarden - **Anxiety Ease** - Anxiety Ease was formulated to help calm the tension of stress and anxiousness. We can steal back those moments of clarity and confidence by slowing down and inhaling a few drops of Anxiety Ease. At Edens Garden, we hope that if you are suffering from anxiety that you seek help and let Anxiety Ease work as a tool in your life to find lasting peace.

(https://www.edensgarden.com/collections/synergy-blends)

If you are using doTerra Console, ByFaith Anxiety, EdensGarden anxiety Ease, or any other brand of essential oil singles or blends in order to calm down and obtain peace and tranquility, then you are sinning against the Lord Jesus Christ and greatly grieving the Holy Ghost. Why? Because you are not to rely on a physical thing to comfort you, for the word of God says:

15 If ye love me, keep my commandments. 16 And I will pray the Father, and he shall give you another Comforter, that he may abide with you for ever; 17 Even the Spirit of truth; whom the world cannot receive, because it seeth him not, neither knoweth him: but ye know him; for he dwelleth with you, and shall be in you. 18 <u>I will not leave you comfortless: I will come to you.</u> (John 14) (Emphasis Added)

What is so different about using essential oils in order to calm down, or taking a shot of whiskey, a glass of wine, or a few beers? Either way you are substituting chemicals in order to do the job that ought to be done by going to the Lord Jesus Christ in prayer and being filled with the Holy Spirit.

Besides, whether you use essential oils, booze, or drugs, none of those things can, nor will they ever be able to comfort you. Why? Because the word of God states:

3 Blessed be God, even the Father of our Lord Jesus Christ, the Father of mercies, and the God of all comfort; 4 Who comforteth us in all our tribulation, that we may be able to comfort them which are in any trouble,

169

> by the comfort wherewith we ourselves
> are comforted of God. 5 For as the
> sufferings of Christ abound in us, so
> our consolation also aboundeth by
> Christ. (2 Corinthians 1)

If you block God from working in your life by seeking and numbing your anxiety through witchcraft, booze, or any other method, then you will stagnate in your Christian growth and become useless for God. The Lord wants to use you for his glory, and for his glory is why you were created.

> 11 Thou art worthy, O Lord, to
> receive glory and honour and power:
> for thou hast created all things, and
> for thy pleasure they are and were
> created. (Revelation 4)

The Lord will allow trials to come into your life so you will learn to lean on the Lord Jesus Christ and grow as a Christian. Then somewhere down the road of life the Lord will be able to use you to minister to somebody who will be going through the trials that you are going through right now.

At that time you will have the privilege to minister and be used by the Lord. But if you use the Essential oils to obtain an escape from the trials, then you will never be what the Lord Jesus Christ wants you to be for Him. You are not letting

170

Him work in your life. To use the following oils for what they claim to accomplish in a person, takes zero self-denial, it takes zero faith, it takes zero confession of sins, it takes zero prayer, and it takes zero amount of standing on the promises of the word of God! These oils are not of faith, and whatsoever is not of faith is sin!

Notice the following essential oils and what they are intended for:

Young Living - Forgiveness™ contains an aroma that supports the ability to forgive yourself and others while letting go of negative emotions, an important part of personal growth.

(https://www.youngliving.com/en_US/produc ts/forgiveness-essential-oil)

Young Living - Hope - The blend of essential oils found in Hope™ brings an aroma that invites you to restore your faith by reconnecting with feelings of strength and stability.

(https://www.youngliving.com/en_US/produc ts/hope-essential-oil)

doTerra - Forgive - The fresh, woody aroma of doTERRA Forgive Renewing Blend helps to counteract emotions of anger and guilt, while

171

promoting the liberating feelings of contentment, relief, and patience.

Are you carrying a burden that grows heavier with time? Would you be better off just letting it go and facing a future unfettered by anger and guilt? When you are ready to move forward, doTERRA Forgive Renewing Blend of tree and herb essential oils will help you discover the liberating action of forgiving, forgetting, and moving on. Start each of your tomorrows relieved and contented with Forgive Renewing Blend.

(https://www.doterra.com/US/en/p/forgive-renewing-blend-oil)

doTerra - PastTense - PastTense is a distinctive blend of essential oils known to help provide grounding and balanced emotions. Known for their soothing effects on both the mind and body, the essential oils in PastTense quickly, promote feelings of relaxation and calm emotions.

(https://www.doterra.com/US/en/p/pasttense-oil)

(Notice the number of times "You" is used.)

Edens Garden - Shine - You'll
love Shine by Edens Garden if you like Elevation by doTERRA. Whether you can feel it or not, you are worthy of goodness. You are worthy of love, kindness and hope. When you believe in yourself, you can float. You rise above the pettiness and lackluster moments. Shine synergy blend helps you grab ahold of the sparkle you already possess.

(https://www.edensgarden.com/collections/synergy-blends/products/shine)

I hate to wake you up from your fairy tale, but according to the word of God, life is not about you! The word of God states,

11 Likewise reckon ye also yourselves to be dead indeed unto sin, but alive unto God through Jesus Christ our Lord. (Romans 6)

24 Then said Jesus unto his disciples, If any man will come after me, let him deny himself, and take up his cross, and follow me. (Matthew 16)

Aromatherapy

It is no surprise to find that self is magnified with the use of essential oils, for at the heart of aromatherapy is witchcraft, which is a work of the flesh. You, you, self, self, body, body, I love me, I really love me!

These are obviously just a few of the many, many blends of essential oils. By the descriptions they are very dangerous spiritually. They are portrayed as a substitute for the working of the Holy Spirit. It is very very plain that the use of essential oils goes DIRECTLY AGAINST the Holy Spirit. It ought to be the convicting power of the Holy Spirit that moves you to forgive. It ought to be the Holy Spirit through the word of God that brings hope. It ought to be the Comforter who comforts you when you are down. And it ought to be the Holy Spirit that convicts you into realizing that you are not good, and you definitely cannot believe in yourself.

3 For we are the circumcision, which worship God in the spirit, and rejoice in Christ Jesus, and have no confidence in the flesh. (Philippians 3)

To use these physical things for the intended outcome of spiritual fruits is not of faith, and grieves the Holy Spirit.

Yes, there are times when physical things are used in proper medicine. Pain killers, anesthesia, as well as intubation and other medical procedures that save lives and ease the debilitating effects of pain. Those activities are strictly limited to the physical body and are not against the word of God.

> **31 And Jesus answering said unto them, They that are whole need not a physician; but they that are sick. (Luke 5)**

Jesus Christ recommended physicians, just make sure the physician you go to is the one God wants you to go to. No, they are not God. You have to pray your way through your treatments, but the nature of the treatments in evidence based western medicine is not contrary to the word of God. It is the Eastern Mystical spirit based medicine that is against the word of God, of which aromatherapy is included.

Do you know why there are so many blends of essential oils that are concerned with Peace, Calm, Rest, Hope, Joy, and conversely Anxiety, Fear, Troubled, and such like? It is because when you use witchcraft you open a door into your body, mind and spirit. **Through that door enters an unclean spirit that is agitated, fearful, sad, depressed, and everything that the fruits of the Holy Spirit are not!**

So even though you may be born again, by doing what the witches do when they practice witchcraft you open a door and let an unclean spirit enter your body. In your flesh now dwells an unclean entity. That unclean spirit then quenches the Holy Spirit, and brings out fruits in the life of the Christian that are "against" the Holy Spirit. On top of that is the conviction of the Holy Spirit that you are not in fellowship with God, and the conviction that you are not right with God.

It really isn't hard to see that these oils are wrong. For someone who is open to the truth, it really doesn't take this many pages to see that aromatherapy is against God. All you have to do is see what the witches do with the essential oils, or incense, when they practice witchcraft. To any honest Christian that alone should cause enough doubt to quit doing whatever actions/works of aromatherapy you have been doing.

Let me repeat, those who don't repent but work with this witchcraft get defiled and take on an unclean spirit. Instead of bringing forth the first fruit of the Holy Spirit, which is love, the fruit of an unholy spirit is brought forth which most likely is hate. You will have emotions of hatred like you never had them before. Often times this hatred will be vented upon your spouse, loved ones, or other Christians.

It is obvious from the scriptures that if a person is filled with the Holy Spirit, emotions, and actions take place that are direct outpourings through you of the Holy Spirit.

18 And be not drunk with wine, wherein is excess; but be filled with the Spirit; (Ephesians 5)

22 But the fruit of the Spirit is love, joy, peace, longsuffering, gentleness, goodness, faith, 23 Meekness, temperance: against such there is no law. (Galatians 5)

The nine fruits of the Holy Spirit cannot be faked. You either have them to a greater or lesser degree, or you do not.

It can also be expected that if you are filled with an unclean spirit, then the emotions and characteristics of that unclean spirit will manifest themselves through you as well. The characteristics of unclean spirits are given in the gospel of Mark 5, as well as other places in the gospels. As a general overview, unclean spirits are fearful (especially of Jesus Christ), depressed, crying, agitated, rebellious, cannot rest, selfish, loud, religious, preoccupied with death, as well as sick, causing the person to be sick.

Instead of the Holy Spirit produced fruit of joy, there is the unclean spirit fruit of sorrow and depression. Instead of the Holy Spirit fruit of peace, you experience turmoil and nervous anxiety.

177

Instead of the Holy Spirit fruit of long-suffering, the Christian becomes very impatient. Instead of gentleness, the Christian becomes hard and unmerciful. Instead of goodness, they become hurtful and mean. Instead of bringing forth the fruit of faith, they are consumed with fear and worry. Instead of the fruit of meekness, there is the haughty vaunting of self. Instead of the fruit of temperance, they fail to to control themselves, or as the Bible puts it, they become incontinent.

A Christian in such a case has opened a door. If that is you, dear reader, then you need to repent and destroy all of your oils and books on witchcraft. Any and all things related to witchcraft must be destroyed and removed from your life and house, You need to pray and ask the Lord Jesus Christ if there is anything else in your house that you need to get rid of, and is there anything else in your life that you need to repent of and confess in prayer to the Lord Jesus Christ. By doing this you will have revival in your soul.

If you have been using essential oils, and thus participating in the works of witchcraft, then you are going to be greatly influenced by an unclean spirit and his goal is to bring reproach to the name of Jesus Christ. He wants to kill you spiritually, steal your joy, and destroy your testimony.

10 The thief cometh not, but for to steal, and to kill, and to destroy: I am

come that they might have life, and
that they might have it more
abundantly. (John 10)

Instead of being used by Jesus Christ, you will be
used by Satan to hinder the work of God on this
earth. You may think that you are allright. You
may think that you are ministering for the Lord
Jesus Christ, but you are not.

I was just visiting a church where, the previous
Wednesday evening service (we were not present), a
singing group ministered in song. I was told that
at the vestibule where they had CD's available for
sale, they also had essential oils for sale. They
were being used by Satan to destroy a very good
church.

The word of God is plain in this respect. You are
doing the same things the witches do when they
practice witchcraft. You are doing the works, the
same way the witches do. Keep in mind, when it
comes to healing or emotional correction, you are
doing aromatherapy for the same reasons.

When I was a young boy of nine years old, we
lived somewhat out in the country. The grocery
store was a few miles away. Every now and then
my mother, myself, or my sister, would be cooking.
Maybe pancakes, or a cake or some other recipe. In
the middle of putting the ingredients together we
would realize that we were out of something.
Usually it was eggs, sugar, or not enough flour.

Aromatherapy

In those instances we would go next door to one of our neighbors and ask for some eggs, sugar or flour. Usually they had what we needed, and then returned the ingredients in a few days after going to the store.

In the context of this book the following fictional scenario could very easily take place. It serves as an illustration of what I am writing about.

I present to you Mrs. Ezebel Christian. She is at home with her husband, and it is much like any other day in her life. She knows she is saved. She goes to church and lives, by the worlds standards, a fairly clean Christian life. Some people claim she wears the pants of the house, but we'll save that for another time. The door bell rings, and she wonders, "Who could that be? I wasn't expecting anyone."

Mrs. Ezebel Christian goes to the door and peers through the peep hole and sees her next door neighbor. In her mind flashes the thought, "I wonder what she wants?" Putting on a smile she opens the door to greet her neighbor. Her neighbor, by the way, goes by the name of Scarlet Alchemistress.

"Hello Scarlet, how are you?" Says Ezebel Christian, but I'll just call her Sis. Ezzy.

In reply, Scarlet Alchemistress, a practicing witch, says, "I'm doing well, and I don't mean to bother you, but I was wondering if you could help me?"

Sis. Ezzy replies, "I'll be glad to if I am able.

Won't you come in?" With the invite Scarlet goes into her house. "How can I help you?"

Scarlet begins, "Well, I am getting ready to blend some essential oils for a spell that I want to cast, but I just realized that I am out of frankincense essential oil. I know you don't call them spells, and you don't call it casting, so please forgive me for mentioning that, but it is for the healing of a friend of mine."

"Oh Scarlet," replies Sis. Ezzy eagerly, "I'll be glad to help. Yes, I have some Frankincense that I think you will find very powerful and useful for your spiritual blend."

Scarlet then responds, "It's 100% natural, isn't it? The spell won't work unless it is all natural and pure."

Sis. Ezzy reassuring replies, "Now Scarlet, you know the only essential oils I use are therapeutic grade organic all natural essential oils."

Whith a smile and a nod Scarlet smiles saying, "I thought so. Those are the only kind we witches use as well."

Sis. Ezzy then lowers her voice and jokingly says, as she glances back over her shoulder, "Well, my husband calls me his little witch anyway. (Giggle giggle). By the way, what all are you including in your blend?"

They begin to chatter like two school girls who haven't seen each other for a month.

Scarlet excitedly then explains, "Oh, I am going to

blend frankincense with myrrh, eucalyptus, lemon, and juniper. I will be mindful of the actions as I mix it all together."

Sis. Ezzy replies with an interested look on her face, "You know, Scarlet, I have a blend that is almost identical to what you just described. It is blended by... oh what's the name of that company? Is it bluTerra, or is it mad living? No no, I think it is Paradise Garden. Well, anyway it is almost the exact same thing that you are blending." She then gives her the frankincense.

Scarlett Alchemistress declares as she leaves saying, "Oh Ezebel, thank you so much. I wasn't going to be able to do my witchcraft spell if you hadn't been here for me. Praise the goddess Diana! Do you mind if I replace this frankincense with some from my supply store? It 100% natural and organic just like yours. The name is 666 Full Moon, but the oil is just like yours. As a matter of fact I heard the source is the same as bluTerra!"

Sis. Ezzy replies, "Oh Scarlett, sure that will be fine. When you bring it I will be so excited to hear how it worked. Maybe we can spend some more time and have an oily talk."

Scarlet enthusiastically remarks, "Yes, that sounds like a lot of fun! Again thank you Ezzy, and merry part."

There is no difference in what the witches do, and what the "Christians" do when they practice aromatherapy.

Chapter 8

Camouflage

For almost ten years I worked for a copy service in Modesto, California. We would go to hospitals and doctors offices to copy medical records for attorneys who had clients that had been injured in various ways. Car wrecks, and workman's compensation were very common causes for the litigation. Along with those incidents were slips and falls, as well as sickness and many other reasons for going to court.

Some of the stories I will never forget. The specific information was and may still be private, but in general there were some stories that stood out.

I remember one family that was going on vacation. They were going camping. After loading their things into the pickup truck, they headed out, no doubt excited as they proceeded early in the morning on this, their first day of vacation.

Their young daughter, under ten years old, was allowed

to ride in the back of the truck, which had a camper shell on it. After an hour of traveling they stopped for a bite to eat. They opened the back of the camper and saw that their daughter was asleep, so they left her there in the cool, not cold, to sleep.

Coming back from breakfast she was still sleeping so they headed a couple more hours up the road to where they were going to camp. Almost to the camp ground they stopped at a small country store for some things, and went to the back to get their daughter out, but she did not move.

Sensing something was wrong, they climbed in and found that she was dead. Carbon monoxide from the tail pipe had been entering and filling the back of the truck with poisonous fumes and killed their daughter. I never have forgotten the picture that formed in my head of two young parents whose excitement and anticipation was turned to horror and sadness.

There was another story where a teenage girl had not been feeling well. It was late morning, and she had stayed home from school. Her mother was leaving for a few minutes to go to the store to get some groceries. As she was leaving she looked into her bedroom and saw her daughter sitting on the edge of the bed panting and leaning forward.

Her mother looked at her and asked, "Are you alright?" To which her daughter responded, "Yes, it just feels better when I do this." "Well, alright. I will be back in a few minutes."

When her mother returned the daughter was dead on the floor in front of the bed.

I remember one patient, whose medical records I was asked to copy for further medical care. It was a stack of paper medical charts about one and a half to two feet high. That patient had been in the hospital at least once every year for the past fifteen or so years, and in each of the admissions was for an operation of some sort.

It had a way of making me realize how good I have it!

As I worked for that copy service, some of the medical offices I would go into were Chiropractors. In the Chiropractors' offices were charts and things on the walls about Chiropractic treatment.

One of the words of wisdom "sayings" that was on the walls was something like this. Try everything you can naturally first, and then if you still need help, go see a traditional doctor. That sounds wise doesn't it! That really makes sense. Start with the least invasive treatments and progress to the final step which is going to a traditional doctor.

There are some problems though with this philosophy. First of all, the natural treatments are not true science, but science falsely so called. (1 Tim. 6:20) That is why there are explanations and charts on the walls of how it "works." The second problem with that philosophy is you will first be dabbling in meta-physical medicine, which is witchcraft.

You see, meta-physical is outside of the physical realm. It is in the spiritual realm and thus it is spirit medicine. I most certainly don't mean the Holy Spirit either!

There is also a third problem that takes place when this philosophy is accepted.

The spirit realm is very real! If you are saved and believe the Bible, then you ought to know that!

> **12 For we wrestle not against flesh and blood, but against principalities, against powers, against the rulers of the darkness of this world, against spiritual wickedness in high places. (Ephesians 6)**

You would think that Christians would take things like this much more seriously, but for the most part they don't; especially those who believe the King James 1611 is the inerrant word of God. The attitude with many born again Bible believing Christians is that they are untouchable. Little do they know that the spiritual wickedness has beguiled them in many ways.

The spirit realm is very real, and it is very powerful. A Christian is protected by the Lord Jesus Christ when they get saved. Your salvation is perfect, and your name is written in the Lamb's book of life. If you are saved and truly born again, then you are not going to Hell. Be keenly aware that does not mean you are immune from the fiery attacks of the Devil. The Bible states that you are in a spiritual battle.

So, you are protected by the Lord from attack, unless the Lord allows Satan to attack you, as He did with Job. There are times He allows this, and He has his reasons. But there is another way that Satan can attack you, which is if you open a door for him to walk through. You can open the door knowingly, or unknowingly. Either way the door is opened, it allows spiritual wickedness to beguile and attack you.

When a person, saved or lost, goes to meta-physical medical treatments there is a spiritual action that enters their body. It is an unclean spirit. If it is a Christian the first treatment will work, almost miraculously. Whatever the problem was, there will be relief and the Christian goes away marveling at what just took place. The second treatment may work great as well, and the Christian is sold. Then the third treatment doesn't work. This is excused and an appointment is set up for a fourth time.

Little by little the treatments don't seem to work like they did the first and second time. Discouragement begins to overtake the patient when they try it one more time, and almost miraculously it works again. The Christian is being played with. This unclean spirit then begins to manipulate the body for his purposes.

Time goes by and the health of the patient continually gets worse. The natural organic treatments just don't seem to be working anymore and the discomfort is such that they decide they are going to a traditional doctor to see if that can help. Now however, there is a problem. That unclean spirit is going to work!

The patient goes to the real medical doctor, and maybe they run tests, take x-rays, and conduct various other tests to determine what the problem is. When the tests come back, the doctor looks at all of the information and tries to come up with a diagnosis but can't seem to get a definite one.

He then tries one thing after another, but nothing really works as it should. He then tries something else, but it doesn't work either. The appearance comes across that the traditional doctor doesn't know what he is doing, and in such a situation he doesn't.

What is happening is the unclean spirit that resides in the body is camouflaging symptoms and tests so as to confuse the doctor and make him look like a fool. Then, the patient returns to the meta-physical witch doctor and the treatment works. The reply comes, "Traditional doctors...they don't have a clue as to what they are doing!" The unclean spirit just won a great victory in the beguiling of the patient, as well as the destruction of their body and health.

It is very very very common, that the people using holistic medicine are the sickest people around! Amen and amen!

Recently I heard the story of a man who had liver cancer. The prognosis was not good. He went to church and asked for the church to pray over him, which they did. A few days later he attended a Bible study. There at the Bible study a man was visiting and asked the cancer patient if he would let him pray over him as well. The man with the cancer agreed, and as the visitor prayed over him he experienced a very real entity come out of his mouth. As it did all he could do was roar like a hideous creature. After that night, the cancer patient went back to the doctor and the cancer was gone.

Do I believe that happened? Yes, I have no reason not

to. Do I believe all sickness is Satanic? No, I do not! Do I believe someone is not right with God if they are sick? No, I do not! But somewhere in the past of that man's life, he opened a door. Maybe through music, movies, or other occult practices, and an unclean spirit entered his body.

After the prayer, that entity probably left, though you can only believe the word of God, not a supernatural manifestation. Either way, if that man did not repent of the sin that he had committed, then chances are the entity will return, and it will be much worse.

> 24 When the unclean spirit is gone out of a man, he walketh through dry places, seeking rest; and finding none, he saith, I will return unto my house whence I came out. 25 And when he cometh, he findeth it swept and garnished. 26 Then goeth he, and taketh to him seven other spirits more wicked than himself; and they enter in, and dwell there: and the last state of that man is worse than the first. (Luke 11)

What's the problem? You opened a door, became deceived, in-dwelt by an unclean spirit, and it's all downhill from then on. But it seemed so innocent and natural. It seemed so right, and it sounded so good. You believed a lie, JUST AS EVE DID!

She looked and saw that it was good for food. She saw that it was pleasant to the eyes. After all, it was desired to make one wise, so she took, and died spiritually. So will you. You will die spiritually when you get into metaphysical treatments.

Your Bible reading will be dead. Your prayer life will die. And the conviction from the Holy Spirit will cease if you don't repent and get out of the metaphysical medicine. The works of your flesh will go directly against the Holy Spirit.

This is why I asked you earlier in this book, how long has it been since you were under conviction? How long has it been since you were broken in prayer to the Lord Jesus Christ? How long has it been?

If you have been using essential oils, Aromatherapy, Acupuncture, Yoga, and any number of the other metaphysical treatments out there, then you need to repent, remove everything from your house that is associated with it and burn it all, just like they did in Acts 19 with their curious arts.

Chapter 9

Plug-in Witchcraft

What? You have got to be kidding! Air-freshener plug-ins?

Remember that Galatians has to do with the works of witchcraft and one of the works of witchcraft is aromatherapy. There is no doubt about that. Aromatherapy is listed in the courses of study to get a degree in witchcraft. Aromatherapy is described over and over in the witchcraft supply stores as well as on the websites of witches when they describe the works of witchcraft. There is zero doubt that the witches practice aromatherapy as part of their witchcraft.

When the witches use aromatherapy and essential oils they infuse the oils into the air. How do they do this? Usually they warm the oils with a candle, a light bulb, or electronically with an infuser or atomizer. One way or another they get the oils/scents floating around in the air.

For others they use aromatic incense such as the

Aromatherapy

Hindus use. Thus aromatic smoke floats in the air. Either way though, scents of plants are infused into the air and are breathed into the nostrils thus placing aromatherapy on a spiritual level.

7 ...God...breathed into mans nostrils the breath of life. (Genesis 2)

Did you get that? It read, "NOSTRILS." Do you know what that means? It means nostrils. The spirit that God placed into man was placed into and through his nostrils. Your spirit is in your nostrils and thus is your breath.

26 ...As the body without the spirit is dead. (James 2)

If you can't breath, guess what happens... you are a dead duck. To infuse scents into the air places aromatherapy on a spiritual level. You are defiling your spirit when you use aromatherapy.

When a witch infuses scents into the air they are attempting to energize the air and bring about a spiritual power that they intend to use to bring about what they want to happen. One of the ways they do this is to warm the oils thus causing them to evaporate and infuse into the air.

An air freshener plug-in is plugged into the electrical outlet. Why? So that it will warm the scented oils in the infuser to release them into the air. It gets back to the works of witchcraft. It has to do with the works. One of the works of witchcraft is to infuse scents into the air by warming them and that is exactly what the air freshener plug-ins do. The same way.

Don't forget the god of this world. He uses subtlety, and he has had much experience in these of that subtlety. Eve was blinded to his subtlety, and many of the Christian women today are blinded to it as well. Adam was not blinded to it for the Bible says that,

> **14 Adam was not deceived, but the woman being deceived was in the transgression.**
> (1 Timothy 2)

Many times I have heard lost women mentioned that their husband calls them a little witch, or their little bag of witchcraft. The man will see it when often times the woman will not.

The following stories are first person stories. These stories are from people that I know personally and have been around many times.

These stories have to do with nightmares which began to occur when they started using essential oils, and when they stopped using the essential oils the nightmares stopped at the same time. Along with their stopping the use of the essential oils, they repented and confessed their sin to the Lord Jesus Christ at the same time as well.

Graciously invited out to eat, we sat down with this pastor and his wife. We have known them for about ten years and they have been faithful Christians. He had heard me preach against the New Age Medicine (which is nothing else than old age mysticism), so he knew the dangers of the occult influences associated with the various practices.

As we talked and fellowshipped he mentioned that he had nightmares around four times a week. I thought to myself, "Four times a week? Wow!" Not only that, but his daughter would have the nightmares as well, and it was to the point with her that she would leave a light on at night when she went to bed.

I knew that he was aware of the occult dangers, but I asked him anyway, "What are you doing? Are you using any New Age Medicine?" To this he replied, "No, at least not that I know of." I asked are you using any essential oils, or candles or such? To this he replied that he has air fresheners plugged into the outlets because they have dogs and they don't want the house to smell like dogs.

I then told him that there are essential oils in those diffusers and with the plug in to warm the oils it is not any different than what the witches do. (Remember it is the works of witchcraft, and the works are to warm essential oils so they diffuse into the air.). I told him to get rid of those diffusers and see what happened.

A month or two later I ran into him in town and asked him how things were going. He told me that since getting rid of the diffusers that his nightmares went away for him and his daughter. She can now sleep with the light off.

Pastor D.

Another story is about another pastor who was having nightmares as well. He was not sure about what I was telling him, but he would listen. He had the air freshener plug-ins plugged in his walls. I told him that his nightmares were probably due to the infusers he had in his house. To this he seemed a bit incredulous and doubtful of what I was telling him. So I said, "Well, give it a try." Get rid of them for six months and see what happens.

The next year we came back to this church and were over at his house for food and fellowship. Amidst the conversation he said that he took my advice and it worked. I had forgotten what I had told him, so I asked, "What advice?" He then refreshed my memory and told me that he pulled out all of the plug-in air fresheners and his nightmares went away.

Aromatherapy

Chapter 10

What Should I do?

If you have read the evidence presented and have been practicing aromatherapy and the use of essential oils then you need to repent.

You have unknowingly opened a door to unclean spirits. My wife and I did the same thing as well. The key to victory is to repent and close the door. What does that mean? To repent is to change your mind about a thing.

If you are born again, then there came a time when you changed your mind about yourself. Up until that time you thought that you were good, or everything was alright between you and God. Then somewhere, somehow, you were presented with the truth of how you had sinned against God, and because of your sins you were lost and on your way to Hell. Along with that realization you found out that the Lord Jesus Christ died for you on the cross of Calvary, and shed his blood a payment for your sins. You knew that you were a sinner, and that Jesus Christ died for you to save you and get you to Heaven.

When you accepted the truth and saw yourself as lost, you repented. With that knowledge and belief, actions followed because of your repentance. You called upon the Lord Jesus Christ for salvation and He saved you. (If you have not done this, the next chapter goes into more detail, and explains salvation.).

So, now dear reader, perhaps you have been involved with aromatherapy and the use of essential oils. In the most basic aspect of this study, there is no doubt that you are doing the same things the witches do, when they practice witchcraft. You are using essential oils the same way, which is infusing them into the air. Also you are using them for the same reasons, which is for healing and emotional correction.

Yes, the witches use them for other things as well, and the witches practice other things as well in their works of witchcraft. Realize that the works you have done in your use of aromatherapy match the works of the witches. This also matches what the word of God states in Galatians 5, that witchcraft is a work of the flesh.

You need to repent of your use of aromatherapy. Yes, you need to repent of your witchcraft, and accept the fact that you have grieved the Lord Jesus Christ for using aromatherapy. You have quenched the Holy Spirit and defiled your body, which is the temple of the Holy Spirit.

If you still do not believe what I am writing in this book, then I give you a challenge. Ask the Lord Jesus Christ if what I have written matches the word of God.

The Bible says, "Let God be true, and every man a liar." (Rom. 3:4). Do not blindly take what I have written, for then you would be following a man. You need to see your actions before the Lord Jesus Christ. That way your actions are based upon conviction between you and Jesus Christ.

I will say, just the mere fact that essential oils are a main product listed in the pagan and witchcraft supply stores ought to be enough evidence to at least make you stop the use of them until you know for sure yes or no. To proceed if you are not sure, is to take a chance of sinning and grieving the Lord Jesus Christ.

Remember also that Jesus Christ wants you to live clean. He wants you to know if these things are wrong or not.

Aromatherapy

Chapter 11

Salvation

Dear friend, would you let me ask you one of the most important questions that you will ever be asked in this life? The question is this, "Do you know that you are going to Heaven when you die?"

Perhaps you say that no one knows where they are going when they die. Well, St. Peter knew that he was going to Heaven for he said that he was born again, "kept by the power of God," and that he had an incorruptible inheritance reserved in Heaven. St. John knew that he was going to Heaven for he said, **"Now are we the sons of God...and we know that we shall be like Him." "These things have I written unto you that believe on the name of the Son of God; that ye may know that ye have eternal life..."** (1John 5:13)

Not only did St. Peter and St. John know where they were going when they died, but St. Paul also knew for he said that he had a **"desire to depart, and to be with Christ; which is far better."** And of course Jesus Christ said, **"I go unto my Father."**

All of these men, as well as the Son of God, knew where they were going when they died. If they knew, you can know also. In the Bible St. John wrote again,

> **13 These things have I written unto you that believe on the name of the Son of God; that ye may know that ye have eternal life...**
> **(1 John 5)**

Do you know that you have eternal life? Do you know that you are going to Heaven when you die?

Let me start at the very beginning. The person you are going to have to deal with is called, "the Word," and He is the Creator of all things.

> **1 In the beginning was the Word, and the Word was with God, and the Word was God. 2 The same was in the beginning with God. 3 All things were made by him; and without him was not any thing made that was made. 4 In him was life; and the life was the light of men. (John 1)**

He is also righteous. In Heaven they worship Him.

> **8 And the four beasts had each of them six wings about him; and they were full of eyes within: and they rest not day and night, saying, Holy, holy, holy, Lord God Almighty, which was, and is, and is to come. (Revelation 4)**

His name is the Son of God, the Lord Jesus Christ.

> 8 But unto the Son he saith, Thy throne, O God, is for ever and ever: a sceptre of righteousness is the sceptre of thy kingdom. (Hebrews 1)

The Lord Jesus Christ is Holy. That means He has never sinned one time. There is no spot nor blemish in the Lord Jesus Christ. He is absolutely perfect. Along with that, Heaven is also perfect. It is a place of joy, happiness, light, and righteousness. In Heaven:

> 4 And God shall wipe away all tears from their eyes; and there shall be no more death, neither sorrow, nor crying, neither shall there be any more pain: for the former things are passed away. 5 And he that sat upon the throne said, Behold, I make all things new. And he said unto me, Write: for these words are true and faithful. (Revelation 21)

This is just a glimpse of Heaven, but it gives a glimpse of a place where it can honestly be written as an epigraph, "...and they lived happily ever after." Doesn't that sound like a place you would like to spend eternity in?

Heaven is beautiful because the God of Heaven is holy, the place called Heaven is holy, and the people of Heaven are holy. My desire in writing this is to tell you how you can know when you die you will make it to this beautiful place called Heaven. Then it can be written of you, he or she lived happily ever after.

This brings us to the subject of holiness. Are you holy? Are you righteous? Are you a good person? To answer the first two questions I would think it would be easy to answer, "No." You are not holy, and you are not righteous. But maybe your answer to the third question is, "Yes." You might say that you are a good person. You're nice to others and try to help folks when you can. That is a good thing.

When it comes to holiness though, how do we judge what is holy? How do we know what holiness is? To answer these two questions we must go back in time about 3500 years to a mountain in Arabia. (Gal. 4:25. The traditional Mt. Sinai that is located in the Sinai peninsula is not the true Biblical Mt. Sinai). It is a mountain called Mt. Sinai. On that mountain is a man called Moses. The Lord God has called him there, and camped below in the plain is a nation God has called out of Egypt named Israel.

The top of that mountain can be seen today in 2017. It is in Arabia and has been burnt black, and is a reminder of the event that I am about to tell you of.

Moses went up onto the mount, and God came down in fire on the top of that mount and gave Moses the Ten Commandments. These Ten Commandments are a glimpse of holiness, or should I say, the standard by which holiness is judged. I am going to use only four of the ten and let's see how you measure up to holiness.

1. 7 Thou shalt not take the name of the LORD thy God in vain; for the LORD will not hold him guiltless that taketh his name in vain. (Exodus 20)

This is the third commandment. To take the Lord's name in vain is called blasphemy and it is very serious. Have you ever taken the Lord's name in vain? In other words have you ever said, "Oh my God," or "Jesus Christ," or "Lord God Almighty," or just "Jesus?"
Have you ever said any of these in vain, or other variations? How many times in your life have you taken His name in vain? In vain would mean that you just said His name without using it in a sentence, thus in vain. Since this is called blasphemy, then you would be called a blasphemer.
If you have broken this commandment then you are a blasphemer.

2. 15 Thou shalt not steal. (Exodus 20)

This is the eighth commandment. Have you ever stolen anything in your life? Stop and think about this. Have you ever, without permission, downloaded any music, or anything that was copyrighted? Have you ever taken something that was not yours? Size does not matter. From a piece of candy to millions of dollars, have you ever stolen something?

Aromatherapy

It doesn't matter what religion you are, for these laws are written on your heart. You know instinctively that it is wrong to take something that is not yours.

What does God call someone who steals? They are called a thief. So then if you have stolen anything you are a thief. You are guilty of breaking God's law when He wrote, **"Thou shalt not steal."**

If you have broken both of these commandments, then you are a blasphemer and a thief. Keep in mind this is only two of the ten commandments.

3. 14 Thou shalt not commit adultery. (Exodus 20)

This is to have sex with someone who is not your spouse, thus it is to have sex outside of marriage.

Jesus, who was God manifest in the flesh, went even farther and stated,

28 "But I say unto you, That whosoever looketh on a woman to lust after her hath committed adultery with her already in his heart." (Matthew 5)

Adultery is now committed in your heart by looking on someone and lusting after them sexually, as well as the physical act of fornicating with someone. Fornication is what it is called when sex is committed outside of marriage. This would include Sodomy. Have you ever done that?

206

If you have, even if just once, then you are an adulterer, or could also be called a fornicator. If you have broken all three of these commandments then you are a blasphemer, thief and a fornicator.

4. 18 "...Thou shalt not bear false witness." (Matthew 19)

Also known as, **"Thou shalt not lie."**

Have you ever told a lie? To speak a false witness is to tell a lie. A witness tells what he or she knows. To be a false witness is to not speak or tell the truth about what you know. Have you ever done that? How many times have you done that in your life? 1 time? 10? 100? 1000? Etc.?

A person who tells lies, is called a liar. Then you are a liar.

If you have transgressed all four of these commandments then you are a blasphemer, a thief, a fornicator and a liar. Do you think God will allow you into Heaven? What kind of place would Heaven be if God allowed blasphemers, thieves, fornicators and liars into it? I'll tell you, it wouldn't be a holy place, and it wouldn't be Heaven.

With just four out of ten commandments, we have had a glimpse of holiness. The Bible states,

12 Wherefore the law is holy, and the commandment holy, and just, and

good."(Romans 7)

14...but I am carnal, sold under sin."
(Romans 7)

The truth of the matter is that you are not holy, nor are you even good, and neither am I. We all are sinners and have broken God's commandments.

The Bible says,

9 Know ye not that the unrighteous shall not inherit the kingdom of God? Be not deceived: neither fornicators, nor idolaters, nor adulterers, nor effeminate, nor abusers of themselves with mankind,

10 Nor thieves, nor covetous, nor drunkards, nor revilers, nor extortioners, shall inherit the kingdom of God. (1Corinthians 6)

8 But the fearful, and unbelieving, and the abominable, and murderers, and whoremongers, and sorcerers, and idolaters, and all liars, shall have their part in the lake which burneth with fire and brimstone: which is the second death. (Revelation 21)

14 And death and hell were cast into the lake of fire. This is the second death.

**15 And whosoever was not found
written in the book of life was cast
into the lake of fire. (Revelation 20)**

If you die right now, according to the word of God,
where will you go? Have you ever told a lie? Then you are
a liar and according to the Bible you will go to the lake
of fire.

Is that where you want to go when you die? If you are
in your right mind then you do not want to end up in the
Lake of Fire for all eternity.

Is there a way to be saved from going to Hell? If you
have been honest with yourself about those four
commandments, then you know that you have broken at
least one of them. The Bible says,

**10 For whosoever shall keep the whole
law, and yet offend in one point, he is guilty
of all. (James 2)**

Then according to the word of God you are guilty of
breaking God's law and thus unable of your own self to
enter Heaven.

In your present condition you will one day stand before
your Creator and Judge who will pronounce the
judgement, "Guilty!" The punishment for you is that you
will be cast into Hell and then later cast into the Lake of
Fire. That is what you deserve, and that is what I deserve
as well, but this is where the good news begins.

Good News

Jesus Christ was God manifest in the flesh. That means Jesus Christ was fully God. He came to this earth being born of the virgin Mary, and became a man. While on this earth He never broke God's law one time. Jesus Christ lived a perfect life according to His law. Jesus Christ is Holy. How do I know this? Because after He was crucified on the cross, our Lord arose from the dead after spending three days and three nights in the heart of the earth.

If Jesus Christ had sinned one time, then He never would have been able to rise from the dead. He would have been just like you and me. But He did rise from the dead and was seen by over 500 people after He arose from the dead.

Jesus Christ saw you long before you were ever around. He saw you and He loved you.

> **16 For God so loved the world, that he gave his only begotten Son, that whosoever believeth in him should not perish, but have everlasting life. (John 3)**

God gave his Son; how? He gave him when Jesus died on the cross as the sacrifice for your sins. Jesus Christ took the punishment of your sins upon Himself, and shed His blood as the perfect payment for your sins. The sins that you committed when you transgressed those commandments have all been paid for.

210

6 For when we were yet without strength, in due time Christ died for the ungodly. 7 For scarcely for a righteous man will one die: yet peradventure for a good man some would even dare to die. 8 But God commendeth his love toward us, in that, while we were yet sinners, Christ died for us. 9 Much more then, being now justified by his blood, we shall be saved from wrath through him. (Romans 5)

While you were a sinner, Jesus Christ loved you and died for you on the cross. He also shed His blood as the payment for your sins, but you must pick up the payment.

23 For the wages of sin is death; but the gift of God is eternal life through Jesus Christ our Lord. (Romans 6)

Wages are given as payment for something that you have worked for. Those commandments that you have broken have earned you death. That is your payment, that is what you have worked for.

A gift is something that you do not work for. A gift is given free of charge after the giver worked to purchase it or to make it. The gift that I am writing about here is eternal life. Do you want to live forever? Do you want to go to Heaven when you die? It is a free gift, but there is one catch. You must receive the Lord Jesus Christ in order to obtain eternal life.

Eternal life is not obtained through baptism, church membership, getting rid of bad karma, or any other works. It is obtained through our Lord Jesus Christ. He is the One that paid the price. You must receive Jesus Christ as your very own personal Saviour.

> **10 He was in the world, and the world was made by him, and the world knew him not. 11 He came unto his own, and his own received him not. 12 But as many as received him, to them gave he power to become the sons of God, even to them that believe on his name: 13 Which were born, not of blood, nor of the will of the flesh, nor of the will of man, but of God. (John 1)**

So how do you receive Jesus Christ? If you can't see Him, feel Him or touch Him, how can you receive Him?

> **13 For whosoever shall call upon the name of the Lord shall be saved." (Romans 10)**

You must pray and ask Jesus Christ to forgive you of your sins; to wash you from your sins in His own blood; and ask Him to come into your heart and save you from your sins.

1 And from Jesus Christ, who is the faithful witness, and the first begotten of the dead, and the prince of the kings of the earth. Unto him that loved us, and washed us from our sins in his own blood. (Revelation 1:5)

Summary:
1. You have broken God's Holy Commands.
Blasphemer, Thief, Fornicator or Liar - Guilty!
Headed for the Lake of Fire.

2. Jesus Christ died for your sins, was buried and three days later arose from the grave proving that He was God manifest in the flesh. He paid for **all** of your sins. Your ticket to Heaven is all paid for, now you must receive Jesus Christ into your heart in order to claim the payment for your sins.

3. You must call upon the Lord Jesus Christ to forgive you of your sins and to wash you in His blood. You must ask the Lord Jesus Christ to come into your heart and save you.

Here is a simple prayer to pray. Remember though, that by faith in what God said, you are talking to Jesus Christ from your heart. Reciting this prayer will not save you. You must realize that you are talking to your Saviour, Jesus Christ. He is the One you need to forgive you and to save you. He promised to save you if you call upon His name and God cannot lie. The best way you know how pray this prayer out loud. Talk to the Lord out loud.

Dear Lord Jesus Christ. I come to you as a sinner who has broken your commandments. I am guilty. I believe you died on the cross and paid for my sins. Please forgive me of my sins. Please wash me throughly in your blood. And dear Jesus, please come into my heart and save me. I don't want to go to the Lake of Fire. Thank you for dying for me on the cross and thank you for saving me. In your name, Lord Jesus, I ask these things, Amen.

If you prayed a prayer like that one and meant it, then according to the word of God you are saved from eternal damnation. I now ask you, "Where are you now going when you die?"

> **13 For whosoever shall call upon the name of the Lord shall be saved. (Romans 10)**

> **37 All that the Father giveth me shall come to me; and him that cometh to me I will in no wise cast out. (John 6)**

These are both prescious promises from the word of God.

Bibliography

Chapter 1
Aromatherapy

1. Red Sea Crossing - Satellite Pg15
http://www.beforeus.com/satellite_redsea.html

2. Red Sea Crossing - Chariot Wheels Pg15
https://wyattmuseum.com/discovering/red-sea-crossing - Significance of the wheels

3. Incense Aromatherapy. Pg16
https://highermindincense.com/our-vision/incense-aromatherapy/

4. Aromatic Medicine - Incense. Pg17
https://aromaticmedicineschool.com

Chapter 2
Laying A Foundation

1. Massage Magazine, October 31, 2011/ issue #186
https://www.massagemag.com/aromatherapy-incense-an-ayurvedic-tradition-10022/

Aromatherapy

2. Witchschool. Pg35
http://www.classes.witchschool.com/course.asp

3. Athame Pg36
http://www.theofficialwitchshoppe.net/index.php?mai
n_page=index&cPath=7

4. Spiritual Spells. Pg37
http://www.spiritualspells.com/oils-book.html

5. The Kitchen Wiccan. Pg39
https://www.kitchenwiccan.com/witchs-
cupboard/apothecary/

6. Dark Hollar Witch. Pg40
https://darkhollarwitchcraft.wordpress.com/2014/08
/21/whats-in-your-candle-wax/

6. Scott Cunningham. Pg40-41
http://www.controverscial.com/Scott%20Cunningha
m.htm

7. The Power of scent. Pg41-43
Magical Arometherapy: The Power of Scent, Scott
Cunningham, 1989, Llewellyn Publications

Chapter 3
Quintessential

1. Fifth Element. Pg45
https://www.treehugger.com/health/13-essential-oils-and-what-theyre-good.html

2. Orientation of Pentagram. Pg46
https://www.thoughtco.com/pentagrams-4123031, by Catherine Beyer, Updated October 24, 2017

3. Qibo and The Yellow Emperor. Pg48
DEFILED, Every Word Publishing, Ken McDonald, pg 130

4. Bombastus Paracelsus von Hohenheim. Pg49
https://www.oilsandplants.com/paracelsus.htm

5. Distillation. Pg50
The Essential Oils - Vol. 1: History - Origin in Plants - Production - Analysis, Fred Guenther, Jepson Press, March 15, 2007, ISBN-13: 978-1406703658

6. Quinta Essentia. Pg50
Paracelsus: An Introduction to Philosophical Medicine in the Era of the Renaissanc, 2nd, revised edition, Basel; New York: Karger, 1982, By Walter Pagel, pg 100

7. Contraction of quintessential oil. Pg50
The National Association for Holistic Aromatherapy,

Aromatherapy

https://naha.org/explore-aromatherapy/about-aromatherapy/what-are-essential-oils

8. Webster 1913: Witchcraft. Pg55

9. Why I Quit Karate: Bill Rudge. Pg55
http://www.billrudge.org/why-i-quit-karate

10. Chi in a bottle. Pg56
http://aromaqigong.com/qiblog

11. Palo Santo. Pg56
https://palosantosupply.co/blogs/palo-santo/116334723-your-guide-to-palo-santo-an-introduction

12. Palo Santo Dead 4-10 years. Pg56
https://www.mountainroseherbs.com/products/palo-santo-smudge-sticks/profile

13. Webster 1913: spirit

Chapter 4
Christians Doing Witchcraft

1. doTerra - Forgive. Pg68
https://www.doterra.com/US/en/p/forgive-renewing-blend-oil

2. Young Living - Foregiveness. Pg69
https://www.youngliving.com/en_US/products/forgiv
eness-essential-oil

3. By Faith Oils - Hope. Pg70
https://www.byfaithoils.org/collections/synergy-
blends/products/rejoice-blend-aromatherapy-pure-esse
ntial-oil

4. By Faith Oils. Pg74
https://www.byfaithoils.org

5. American Heritage Dictionary: centering - Pg77-78
American Heritage® Dictionary of the English
Language, Fifth Edition. Copyright © 2016 by Houghton
Mifflin Harcourt Publishing Company. Published by
Houghton Mifflin Harcourt Publishing Company. All
rights reserved

6. Oxford Dictionary: Centering Pg78
https://en.oxforddictionaries.com/definition/centring

7. Witchipedia: Centering. Pg79
http://www.witchipedia.com/def:centering

8. Merriam-Webster: Grounding. Pg80
https://www.merriam-
webster.com/dictionary/grounding

9. Cambridge University: Grounding. Pg80

Aromatherapy

https://dictionary.cambridge.org/us/dictionary/english/grounding

10. Witchipedia: Grounding. Pg81
http://www.witchipedia.com/def:grounding

11. Collins Dictionary: Shielding. Pg86
https://www.collinsdictionary.com/us/dictionary/english/shield

12. Wicca.con: Shielding. Pg86
https://wicca.com/celtic/wicca/defense.htm

13. Joelles Sacred Grove: Protection. Pg87
http://www.joellessacredgrove.com/Herbs/ghijk-herbs.html

14. Young Living: Sacred Mountain. Pg87
https://www.youngliving.com/en_US/products/sacred-mountain-essential-oil

15. Empower Your Oils: Shielding. Pg87
https://www.empoweryouroils.com/single-post/2017/06/02/The-Oil-of-Shielding

List of sites
with description and web address

13 Moons

1. https://www.13moons.com - Since 1997 we have been serving you the very best in magical products!

We have been joined by many home based crafters to bring you unique products; from robes, candles, ritual kits, incense, herbs from our own herb gardens, and much more. Throughout these years we have become intertwined by wonderful people and many places.

In the beginning, we drew a rune symbol on a rock with wishes and desires.

It was cast into the water along with many other elements such as brother wind, sun, moon... and our wishes and desires began to be known to us... and is now 13 Moons. We thank the elements and we thank you for helping us begin a dream and to grow from the Chesapeake Bay in Maryland to beautiful Vermont.

Joelles Sacred Grove

2. http://www.joellessacredgrove.com -
Joelles Sacred Grove: Welcome to my grove!
Kick off your shoes, relax, and make
yourself at home. At this site you'll find lots
of Celtic and Wiccan information, Herb lore,
Candlemaking Instructions and plenty of
other goodies. Whether you've already
found your path or are still searching,

I hope you find something here that will
be of help.

Goddess Isis Books & Gifts

3. http://store.isisbooks.com - Isis
Books - Goddess Isis Books & Gifts is
celebrating 36 years as the premier
metaphysical source on the world-wide-web
and in Denver, Colorado. At Isis Books, all
world spiritual traditions and healing
methods are honored as we seek to bring
ancient wisdom into the modern world.

Part library, part apothecary and part
temple, we provide all the tools for your
soul's journey. Books, music, oracles,
crystal singing bowls, Native American
drums, sacred art and statuary, herbs,
precious oils, crystals, hand- made jewelry

from around the world.....At Isis, we have everything from Angels to Zen! From the curious seeker to the dedicated practitioner, everything a person might want to create their own personal connection with the Divine and explore the world's fascinating traditions can be found here.

Isis is named for, and dedicated to, the ancient Egyptian Goddess Isis - the Goddess of healing, magick, fertility and rebirth.

Witchesofthecraft

4. https://witchesofthecraft.com - Essential oils description was authored by Lady of the Abyss. Posted on July 2, 2015 by ladyoftheabyss

Posted in Articles, Daily Posts, Oils & Ointments

Eclectic Artisans

5. https://www.eartisans.net - Eclectic Artisans is a Pagan marketplace specializing in Wiccan supplies and Pagan products. Explore and discover unique spell supplies, altar supplies, ritual tools, spell

kits, spell candles, books on paganism, pagan jewelry, God and Goddess statuary and much more!

Alchemy-works

6. http://www.alchemy-works.com - Whether you practice witchcraft, ritual magick, or simply enjoy unusual incense, oils, herbs, and seeds, you will find something here of interest. All of our products have traditionally played a role in ancient or modern Earth-based spirituality (Paganism) and magic; many are traditionally used in witchcraft and sorcery. You can learn how to create a spiritual garden, which plants are linked to which planets or aspects of the divine, and how each botanical has been used in a spiritual context, be it spells, rituals, or worship. The informational links can show you paths to further develop your wortcunning.

By Faith Essential Oils

7. https://www.byfaithoils.org - Our Purpose is to Serve our Lord Jesus:

By Faith Essential Oils are bottled and distributed through By Faith Massage Therapy PLLC - Headquartered in

Weatherford, Texas. We are a professional aromatherapy / massage therapy clinic that began buying oils directly from the best small farms and distilleries in the world after being unable to find any company on the market which met our high standards for quality at reasonable prices.

We are a Christian small busniess that never had intentions of getting into the bottling and sales of essential oils. Every step our success was not of our own doing, but a result of the fact that we had given our company to the Lord. In turn, we are making sure to keep the company His.

100% of the profits from all sales on ByFaithOils.org are donated directly to Christian charities.

Selah Essential Oils

8. https://www.selahessentialoils.com - (1) Everyone needs salvation because we all have sinned. Romans 3:10-12, 3:23

(2) The Price (or consequence) of sin is death. Romans 6:23

(3) Jesus Christ died for our sins. He paid the price for our death. Romans 5:8

(4) We receive salvation and eternal life through faith in Jesus Christ. Romans 10:9-10, 10:13 and John 3:16

(5) Salvation through Jesus Christ brings us into a relationship of peace with God. Romans 5:1, Romans 8:1

(6) John 14:26

(The above Plan of salvation was on the Selah website after a lengthy good article.)

Edens Garden

9. https://www.edensgarden.com - When I founded Edens Garden, I knew I wanted to create a company that meant something. After almost a decade of working in the natural industry, I saw that there was a need for an essential oil company that had genuine concern for customers and offered affordable products without compromising on quality....

The medicinal and healing qualities of essential oils are a reminder that God gave us most everything we need for wholeness and health on this earth.

Hope Well Oils

10. https://hopewelloils.com - In 2004 our family learned about using essential oils, and as we shared our experiences with others, we were encouraged by those shopping in our store to source high-quality oils ourselves, thus cutting out the expenses associated with sourcing them from the multilevel marketing company we'd been introduced to. We prayed about this seemingly impossible task, and the Lord opened doors we never realized existed to enable us to confidently begin to source high-quality oils and blend them ourselves.

doTerra

11. https://www.doterra.com/US/en - Founded in 2008, doTERRA was built on the mission of sharing therapeutic-grade essential oils with the world. Having seen for themselves the incredible benefits that can be had from using these precious resources, a group of health-care and business professionals set out to make this mission a reality. They formed a company and named it doTERRA, a Latin derivative meaning "Gift of the Earth."

NOW Foods

12. https://www.nowfoods.com - Even when healthy foods and natural supplements weren't mainstream, NOW's founder Elwood Richard started his own company to meet consumer needs for health foods by offering affordable, high quality natural products. Still family owned 50 years later, NOW has never wavered from this mission.

Young Living Essential Oils

13. https://www.youngliving.com/en_US - Through the painstaking steps of our proprietary Seed to Seal production process, we produce the best essential oils in the world. We are committed to providing pure, powerful products for every family and lifestyle, all infused with the life-changing benefits of our essential oils.

Nature's Sunshine

14. www.naturessunshine.com/us/ - 45 YEARS AGO, Gene and Kristine Hughes became herbal pioneers, planting the seeds that became Nature's Sunshine. Plagued with a nagging stomach condition, Gene started taking cayenne pepper at the

suggestion of a friend. While the herb provided relief, it was difficult to ingest cayenne pepper by the spoonful.

His wife, Kristine, suggested putting the powder into capsules. It was a revolutionary idea—delivering the benefits of herbs through encapsulation. Since becoming the first company to encapsulate herbs in 1972, Nature's Sunshine has grown from a small, family-owned business to one of the leading health and wellness companies in the world.

Plant Therapy

15. https://www.planttherapy.com/our-story - "Our ultimate goal is not to be the largest essential oil company; it is to positively impact the lives of as many people as humanly possible. Ultimately, I feel this is possible only by providing our customers with an exceptional experience that keeps them coming back. By selling such a high quality product at an affordable price, we not only positively affect the lives of our customers, it also gives us the financial means by which we can help those who are less fortunate to live a happier, healthier, and more productive life."

Chapter 5
Dangers Of Using Essential Oils

1. Dr. Yogesh Chandra Tripathi. Pg97
Bio. - Have >32 yrs Res. experience in Plant Sc. with speciality in Phytochemistry. Attained PhD in Chem-Medicinal Chem from BHU, Varanasi, India. Has a strong background in phytochemical study of MAPs & Food plants. Handled projects on basic & applied aspects of phytochemistry, bioprospecting & FRCM with emphasis on high productivity, improved quality & cost-effectiveness. Guided 8 PhD & 18 PG Dissertations; Bagged 29 Best Paper Awards. EB Member/Referee of 15 Journals & LM of 18 Scientific Bodies.
https://www.researchgate.net/post/What_is_the_max imum_number_of_compounds_an_essential_oil_can_cont ain

2. Webster 1913: Refine. Pg98

3. New Yorker Magazine. Pg103
https://www.newyorker.com/magazine/2017/10/09/ how-essential-oils-became-the-cure-for-our-age-of-anxiety   Rachael Monroe

4. Ohio State News. Pg106
https://news.osu.edu/aromatherapy-may-make-you-feel-good-but-it-wont-make-you-well---030308

5. Journal of Psychoneuroendocrinology. Pg107-108
http://www.elsevier.com/wps/find/journaldescription
.cws_home/473/description#description

6. Aromatherapy: Exploring Olfaction: Pg108-109
http://www.yalescientific.org/2011/11/aromatherapy
-exploring-olfaction/

7. Journal of Pediatric Endocrinology and Metabolism.
Pg109-110
(https://doi.org/10.1515/jpem-2015-0248)

8. New England Journal Of Medicine Pg110-111
N   Engl   J   Med   2007;   356:479-   485
DOI:10.1056/NEJMoa064725,https://www.nejm.org/do
i/full/10.1056/NEJMoa064725

9. Merrian-Webster: Endocrine. Pg111

10. Endocrine Society in Chicago:
March 2018 Pg111-112
https://www.forbes.com/sites/brucelee/2018/03/18
/will-essential-oils-like-lavender-and-tea-tree-make-
your-breasts-larger/#4795fbc03fc2

11. Dani Stringer, MSN, CPNP, PMHS. Pg113
https://www.healthline.com/health-news/essential-
oils-hormone-disruption-for-boys#1

11. Vitus agnus cactus: Dr. Kurt Schnaubelt. Pg113
The Healing Intelligence of Essential Oils, Kurt
Schnaubelt, Healing Arts Press, 2011, pg 86

12. Magical Recipes: Dr. R. N. Ashley. Pg114
At The Crossroads - An Essential Truth, Jim Spivey,
1652 Hedrick Mill Rd. Lexington, NC 27292

Chapter 7
Substitutes For Spirituality

1. doTerra: Peace. Pg142
https://www.doterra.com/US/en/pl/proprietary-
blends?q=%3Aname-asc%3Aproductgroup%3Aotgproduc
t%3Aproductgroup%3Aregularproducts%3Aproductgrou
p%3Aretailproduct%3Aproductgroup%3Anotaromatouch
product%3Aproductgroup%3Aonlinevisibleproductgroup
&page=1&sort=name-asc

2. Young Living - Peace and Calming. Pg142
https://www.youngliving.com/en_US/products/c/ess
ential-oil-products/blends

3. By Faith Oils - Tranquility. Pg143
https://www.byfaithoils.org/collections/synergy-
blends

4. 13 Moons - Stress Relief. Pg143
https://www.13moons.com/shop-by-category/essential-oils/oil-blends

5. doTerra - Console. Pg145
https://www.doterra.com/US/en/pl/proprietary-blends

6. By Faith Oils - Anxiety. Pg145
https://www.byfaithoils.org/collections/synergy-blends

9. Edens Garden - Anxiety Ease. Pg145
https://www.edensgarden.com/collections/synergy-blends

10. Young Living - Forgiveness. Pg148
https://www.youngliving.com/en_US/products/forgiveness-essential-oil

11. Young Living - Hope. Pg148
https://www.youngliving.com/en_US/products/c/essential-oil-products/blends

12. doTerra - Forgive. Pg148
https://www.doterra.com/US/en/pl/proprietary-blends

13. doTerra - PastTense. Pg149
https://www.doterra.com/US/en/p/pasttense-oil

14. Edens Garden - Shine. Pg149
https://www.edensgarden.com/collections/synergy-blends?page=2

13670362R00131

Made in the USA
Lexington, KY
02 November 2018